SEP    2016

MW00559652

# Gap Gardening

## Selected Poems

ALSO BY ROSMARIE WALDROP
from New Directions


*Blindsight*

*Curves to the Apple*

*Driven to Abstraction*

*A Key into the Language of America*

*Reluctant Gravities*

*The Reproduction of Profiles*

ROSMARIE WALDROP

# *Gap Gardening*
## *Selected Poems*

Edited by Nikolai Duffy with the author

A NEW DIRECTIONS PAPERBOOK ORIGINAL

Copyright © 2016 by Rosmarie Waldrop
Copyright © 2016 by Nikolai Duffy

All rights reserved. Except for brief passages quoted in a newspaper, magazine, radio, television, or website review, no part of this book may be reproduced in any form or by any means, electronic or mechanical, including photocopying and recording, or by any information storage and retrieval system, without permission in writing from the Publisher.

Grateful acknowledgment is made to the editors and publishers of the books in which the poems of *Gap Gardening* first appeared: *The Aggressive Ways of the Casual Stranger* (Random House, 1972); *The Road Is Everywhere or Stop This Body* (Open Places, 1978); *When They Have Senses* (Burning Deck, 1980); *Nothing Has Changed* (Awede, 1981); *Differences for Four Hands* (Singing Horse, 1984); *Streets Enough to Welcome Snow* (Station Hill, 1986); *Shorter American Memory* (Paradigm Press, 1988); *Peculiar Motions* (Kelsey St. Press, 1990); *A Form / Of Taking / It All* (Station Hill, 1986); *Lawn of Excluded Middle* (Tender Buttons, 1993); *Split Infinites* (Singing Horse Press, 1998); *Love, like Pronouns* (Omnidawn, 2003); and *Splitting Image* (Zasterle Books, 2005). The following books were originally published by New Directions: *The Reproduction of Profile* (1987); *A Key Into the Language of America* (1994); *Reluctant Gravities* (1999); *Blindsight* (2003); *Curves to the Apple* (2006); and *Driven to Abstraction* (2010).

Manufactured in the United States of America
New Directions Books are printed on acid-free paper
First published as a New Directions Paperbook Original (NDP1333) in 2016
Design by Erik Rieselbach

*Library of Congress Cataloging-in-Publication Data*
Waldrop, Rosmarie, author.
[Poems. Selections.]
Gap gardening : selected poems / Rosmarie Waldrop ; edited by Nikolai Duffy with the author.
pages cm
ISBN 978-0-8112-2514-4 (alk. paper)
I. Duffy, Nikolai, editor. II. Title.
PS3573.A4234A6 2016
811'.54—dc23                    2015032661

10 9 8 7 6 5 4 3 2 1

New Directions Books are published for James Laughlin
by New Directions Publishing Corporation
80 Eighth Avenue, New York 10011

FRANKLIN TOWNSHIP PUBLIC LIBRARY
485 DEMOTT LANE
SOMERSET, NJ 08873
732-873-8700

# CONTENTS

*Driven to Abstraction* (2010)

# INTRODUCTION

EDMOND JABÈS HAS COMMENTED how "we always start out from a written text and come back to the text to be written, from the sea to the sea, from the page to the page."[1] There always emerges on the page a blank spot, a blindsight, that experience where, according to the neuroscientist Antonio R. Damasio, a person actually sees more than they are consciously aware of. It is, strangely, an experience of dissociation, vision without visual consciousness. It is analogous to the French term *acousmatique*, which, in the words of the architect Vincent Cornu, denotes "listening to sounds whose origin one cannot see, the acoustic equivalent of indirect lighting."[2]

For Rosmarie Waldrop, writing corresponds to a lens, "a frame wide enough for conjunctions and connotations. And the music of words, with its constant vanishing, to fill in the distance."[3] "My key words," Waldrop writes, "would be exploring and maintaining; exploring a forest not for the timber that might be sold, but to understand it as a world and to keep this world alive."[4] A poem is always in movement, "the way a dancer moves within music."[5]

Throughout Waldrop's connected careers as poet, translator, and publisher, the world is established, tentatively, via a constant negotiation between languages, texts, cultures, histories, between forms and grammars, between familiarity and strangeness, self and other, word and silence, just as, also, it is a negotiation of those more knotty fissures between home and refuge, life and writing, matter and transcendence, tradition and innovation. Waldrop's is a poetry of betweens, of crossings, of differences and relations. Metonymy takes precedence over metaphor; differences become contiguous rather than equivalent. "I enter

1 Edmond Jabès, *The Book of Margins*, trans. Rosmarie Waldrop (Chicago and London: The University of Chicago Press, 1993) 40; quoted in *Lavish Absence*, 109.
2 Vincent Cornu, *In the Thick of Things* (Lewes: Sylph Editions, 2009), 32.
3 Rosmarie Waldrop, "The Ground is the Only Figure," *Dissonance (if you are interested)* (Tuscaloosa: The University of Alabama Press, 2005), 219.
4 Rosmarie Waldrop, "Alarms and Excursions," *The Politics of Poetic Form: Poetry and Public Policy*, ed. Charles Bernstein (New York: Roof Books, 1990), 46.
5 Waldrop, "The Ground is the Only Figure," 232.

at a skewed angle," Waldrop writes in the notebook, "The Ground is the Only Figure," "through the fissures, the slight difference."[6] "Gap gardening," Waldrop calls it, "the unbedding of the always."[7]

Born in Germany in 1935, but resident in the United States since 1958, Waldrop is both an American poet with a continental European accent, and a European poet whose foreignness is one of her principally American characteristics. It is also for this reason that it is difficult to know quite where to place Waldrop: her work shares and develops many of the concerns of the post–second World War American avant-garde but at the same time it does not quite fit neatly into any of the critical molds or theoretical pronouncements of American experimental poetics. Similarly, Waldrop is closely connected to innovative poetries in French and German, but she comes at them, despite her own German roots, at a cultural and linguistic remove. Perhaps it is no surprise, then, that, situated somewhere between America and Europe, one of the central axioms around which Waldrop's poetry turns is the very personal sense that language, the world, can be experienced only as gap or aperture, the stutter of syntax.

In her early poetry Waldrop was interested in exploring the tension between word, line, and silence by complicating the distinction between subject and object. "I propose a pattern in which subject and object function are not fixed, but temporary, reversible, where there is no hierarchy of main and subordinate clauses, but a fluid and constant alternation," Waldrop wrote.[8] Since the 1980s, however, Waldrop's primary form has been the prose sequence. Prose shifts the differences from the outside to the inside. Waldrop is interested in the bluff where prose and poetry meet, or, more properly, where the one falls into the other, prose into poetry and poetry into prose. It is what Waldrop refers to as the "between-genre," such that "the prose paragraph has a spaciousness where form can prove 'a center around which, not a box within which.'"[9]

The poetic sequence becomes the model poetic form. It allows an extended project, commentary, or exposition but it does so without making universal gestures. The episodic quality of the sequence enables disjuncture to become a central part of both the poem's form and content.

6  Ibid., 223.

7  Pam Rehm, quoted by Waldrop in "The Ground is the Only Figure," 242.

8  Waldrop, "Thinking of Follows," 209.

9  Rob Mclennan, "Twelve or 20 Questions with Rosmarie Waldrop," *Rob Mclennan's Blog*, 11 January 2008, http://robmclennan.blogspot.co.uk/2008/01/rosmarie-waldrop-was-born-in-kitzingen.html.

Order is everything. Gesture is a fragile art made of many pieces, the majority of which go unnoticed; it is what Stefan Brecht, in another context, has called a "non-verbal, arational communication," an interlinear interchange.[10] Life is registered formally, like cracks in the pavement, like mortar. "My sequences," Waldrop comments, "make a tease of narrative. They have a narrative structure, but I don't really wrap anything up."[11]

For Waldrop it is the clash of singular, and singularly imperfect, edges that figures the world, in the kind of jarring that exposes loose ends, that gardens the gaps. First and foremost it is a question of finding a form that projects outward, that layers and lays down a topography manifold and open on all sides. It means establishing a poetic method aimed at the adjacent rather than the equivalent. It means finding a way to show, in language, in form, how one perception follows another perception but also how they are not the same and that there is no necessary correspondence, causal or otherwise, between the two. It means "not growing inward, deeper, by finding more to say about the same thing, metaphors for it, symbols, analogies," Waldrop writes, "but instead turning to the adjoining thing, contiguity, further perceptions";[12] it means "exploring the sentence and its boundaries, slidings, the gaps between fragments, the shadow zone of silence, of margins."[13]

The poems in this book span five decades, including poems from each of the eighteen collections Waldrop has published since 1972. They are presented here in chronological order. In interview, Waldrop has commented how continuities, smooth transitions, tend to be false. The sense that one thing follows on from another is bluff, an illusion of order. "There is always," she says, "the feeling that I never have enough information. The process is not so much 'telling' as questioning. This implies interruption. And in the gaps we might get hints of much that has to be left unsaid—but should be thought about.'"[14]

NIKOLAI DUFFY

10  Stefan Brecht, *The Original Theatre of the City of New York: From the Mid-60s to the Mid-70s*, book 1, *The Theatre of Visions: Robert Wilson* (Frankfurt: Suhrkamp Verlag, 1978) 278.

11  Jared Demick, "An Interview with Keith and Rosmarie Waldrop," *The Jivin' Ladybug*, http://mysite.verizon.net/vze8911e/jivinladybug/id53.html.

12  Waldrop, "Charles Olson: Process and Relationship," *Dissonance*, 69–70 [58–80].

13  Waldrop, "Form and Discontent," *Dissonance*, 200.

14  Joan Retallack, "A Conversation with Rosmarie Waldrop," *Contemporary Literature* 40, no.3 (Fall 1999), 341.

# THE AGGRESSIVE WAYS
# OF THE CASUAL STRANGER

*Dark Octave*

*for Edmond Jabès*

To see darkness
the eye withdraws from light
in light
the darkness is invisible
the eye's weakness
is no weakness of the light
but the eye
away from light
is eyeless
its power is not-seeing
and this not-seeing
sees the night
do not dismiss your darkness
or you'll be left
with vision's
lesser angles
it
fills the eye entirely

## Between

*for Ingo*

I'm not quite at home
on either side of the Atlantic
I'm not irritated the fish
kept me
a home makes you forget
unaware
where you are
unless you think you'd like
to be some other place
I can't think I'd like to be
some other place
places are much the same
aware
I'm nowhere
I stand securely in a liquid pane
touched on all sides
to change your country
doesn't make you
grow (a German doll
into an image of America?)
it doesn't make you change so much
you can't remember
I remember
things are much the same
so much the same the
differences are barbed
I try out living at a distance
watching from a window
immobile
not all here
or there
a creature with gills and lungs
I live in shallow water
but
when it rains
I inherit the land

## Like Hölderlin

got up early
left the house immediately
tore out grass
bits of leather in his pockets
hit fences with his handkerchief
answered yes and no
to his own questions

lies under grass
wilted flowers in his pockets
at the fence I pull my handkerchief
he liked to say no
"I'm no longer the same man"
and

"nothing is happening to me"

from *As If We Didn't Have To Talk*

I want to stay and look at
the mess I've made
spills over
context
I'm always on the verge
or seeing it
there
on the edge
of the horizon
with doubt in the foreground
anything may
hence the troubled
periphery
the curve's lost
incomplete
incompletable
wind over the plains abandoned streets
general amnesia the vacant breath of sky
breath of sky
I might as well claim it's a rag to
wipe my hands
but as long as we're
it doesn't matter
in spite of constant variations
what we say

Afterward
the first time lead grey sea
seems to explain
the horizon
exists and doesn't
if I could
find again the precise place
solid
under my foot
but memory
black wind from one place to another
the same oblique
emptiness as
"lived"
space
I don't know why I say all this
except
that openness
within your touch

My memory open
you're there
scenes I'd hardly been aware of
our faces touching
give way to slaughter
of a surprised beast
my body vast
unsure territories
it would take a long
I mean images
what they mean to me gets lost
vibrations
distant heat
it would take a
long walk through mounting sand to reach them
I'm sure I've never known
anything in any
language

The air swollen
moisture
spiderwebs mildewed shadow
if only I could feel real drops
against my lips
spills over the edges
a woman leans out of the window as if there
were anything to see
a hundred yards off
cars race and a jackhammer tears
not even my feet
can hear it
you're walking somewhere
toward me
and in a while we'll
as if things could be touched
teeth against tongue
as if we didn't have to
talk

———

In order not to
disperse
I think each movement of
my hand
turns
the page
the interval has all the rights

The belly of an "a" and
vertigo
throws the words I stand on
into the white
silence charged with
all the
possible rains in the world
go on
fall back on
words always already there
the precise spot
available
as in a fog that
eyes burn
I carry your name away
from our intersection

The years in my face
no spectacular stories adorable
improbabilities
the road just
goes on
without asking
for approval
opaque pulsations
the quality of light not much different
in the distance
it's enough that we're
you don't have to
frenzy of moths close to
while you touch me

———

Nothing started yet
silence holds
my breath
waits to speak
to be able to
open
the essential detour

The way this city plays
with our bodies
so much rain the smell of wet
cement stays in the streets
out of the old shell
we're always walking in a crowd
bookstalls river iron work
on balconies
nothing has stopped over
the years (surprise)
light seems to lean against
absence of gesture
is a move
what's said is out of the game
it hangs on
but that proves nothing
like everyone we adjust
to just those questions
we choose to see
boats on the East River
barges on the Seine
garbage in the Seekonk
float on into the sky
in my dreams too we walk
along the roadless widening
angle of light
or run
legs spider long
breath in our ears
driven by some force again
and again
to the same sentences

Air rises
blue
irresistible with distance
place to stay
immobile
a long time
at the edge of

———

The room's no longer
dissolves in a rhythm from
inside my eye
what we just started to talk of
water seems to rise black and insistent
boats take off
lights grow small
talk
is so difficult
two pairs of eyes
see
two different initial
questions too
disappear
as in a dream
the body
thinks against itself

No slush across the page yet
"my" words
drop of the Allegheny when
the Ohio takes it
the mask of context evaporates
in a mild winter
the spectacle is elsewhere
I need a book to say
I love you
the curtain goes up on
your face
turns toward me on the pillow
contracts and crossfades
into your other larger
dilated pupils no longer search
across the impersonal
meaning there's nothing
my body hides that
you don't know about

As if nothing had
started yet
energy of beginning pushes toward
my life ahead somewhere
interval difficult
to close no matter
how I curve
the questions I
live in are always too big
I'm not talking about
violent wind blows the mind empty
new beginnings nor our
walking toward where our horizons
for an instant
overlap but where
I could get into my story
the road catches
up with itself and I'll
be where I haven't left

# THE ROAD IS EVERYWHERE,
## OR STOP THIS BODY

Exaggeration of a curve
exchanges
time and again
beside you in the car
pieces the road together
with night moisture
the force of would-be sleep
beats through our bodies
denied their liquid depth
toward the always dangerous next
dawn bleeds its sequence of ready signs

a question of
no just a cigarette frays
analogies out of
too frequent a departure
leaves only an ash
of memory itches for words
in my mouth won't be born into
tranparency no longer open
before me
accelerates
into solid illusion
so I try to shift or at least
talk
the road comes back to the surface
in spite of the cigarette
licks my lips
two horns
and a field blown with
wildflowers withdraw
(gesture?) I don't
like the car herds move through our caves
and the life I thought mine passes
by an inch
the extreme tips of
my expectations

time's skin shrinks under
these 2000 pounds of metal
knot villages and fields and
rivers into repetition
explodes
eyeballs windshields
onto a distance
slopes off the air
around nerve lost
would make

crash across
my weight
still untransparent
in beat with the explosions
not talked about
deafen

can I add more than
100 simultaneous miles of

presence every
day shifts unceasingly
parallel bodies
obliquely conscious of
larger and larger blue or grey slabs of air
squeeze through the ventilator
widen the angle of
my look digests field
after field of the "world"
till my eyes fat as butter bloat
outlines
into threshold

smell of fresh grass sails through
the years harden
between you and
your language shields (you thought) against time's
arrows pierce the lungs of
some giant faceless beast with
missing eyes beyond
the range of
pronouns snare us centaurs
half car half man
and what you took for granted
rises from the wrong end
of a sentence and from then on

it's

    after ◄ DETOUR

through the slums of possibles

batteries plunged in their own
acid erodes the
consonants cut in on vowels
before they can fade in
the air makes way for illusion of depth
streaks the (possible)
spectator into grey blur of
a squirrel?
disguises
the lack of more than
two dimensions
roar into view

the difference between here and
here "simple" extension
rushes into
the blare of a horn
would rip the air accompanies
the tissue of pleasure inside
pleasure
the ground swells the
double sheet of the
way back of
the outside rises up
into the bright blue sky
off balance

now a different economy would
balance
never happens without words
spill down into
the levels in between
my sex and the beginning
of a cycle skin signs and
obliterates in
the same tumescence
carries the words across
my very blood
rolls through the pages toward
void suddenly of our language
a light
flows like ink

*for Otto Graf*

curve

of a present perfect twisted
might
continue backward beyond
the "point"
belongs to no one
is as fuzzy as
beginnings recede to
deeper lairs
won't fossilize the embryo "we
have never had"
an edge on passage
steams up my corvair's window
and something
doesn't get said

cars simulate
the ambiguity of stone with
compact outsides
cave
into hollows
our rites abolish
distance as tombs were thought to
but metals conduct faster
and without decay
opaque vibrations from old immobility
amplify
the constant small change
in our cells

behind your
eyes on the ambush of interest
unravels this rolling system of
diminishing utility invents
new happinesses
in time intensity and mostly
prices bridle the movement
as gravity ("just
the right amount" he said) would pull
your impulse down to
metal ploughs deeper
into a sharper space
the rapid shift into a

probes the viole(n)t sky

oscillating
between middletown connecticut and
providence rhode island
the always open
circulation grows with the prices
train the eye on
opaque metal
the slower language of
dust softens the horizon
recedes no farther
than shifts in the spectrum
the waves
the blue bodiless shock of the air

200 miles of nerve per hour with the guardrails down
can churn the intermittent
shapes into sheer
bodies touch there's no
question why
my tongue on your
speed leaps ahead of
he will come on a stallion
he will come on the power and
fury of wind races
out beyond calculating the

of soil of labor of investments into
the warp toward a dimension
we don't yet have
opens layer after
layer pushes past speech

*for Charles Hine*

halfway between false exit
and spectators swarm up
into the old texts strut out
of our crystal ball
as if the future had to be
remembered words
as in a prison
when head-on into
speed
is the evidence
we have prepared
from sperm and egg
to spring into the muscled current
sweeps through
roads connect all tongues

locked into my own momentum
could bang bone
against bone but just
shoots by the

**SCENIC OVERVIEWS**

busy and deroute me in
changing relays
the future works complexities into
my optical concessions
blend real surfaces
with the illusion of
deep space and solid
paper consumes
all representation back
into force and field

it's not enough to think to see

shock of the "outside" at our
fingertips
radiate a cone of attention
through the steering wheel out into
points of space my body
haunts from inside
the "world" is not ahead where I'm
launched into the gap
of mind ahead of body
widens with the metal lining of
my skin
flaunts its refusal
to harden into
durability

the signs
of course I want this sequence

won't get me out I
participate in spite
of me
if I look back
there's no trace
of my passage
no improbable footprint
or tire mark
sitting in my own obstacle
eyes open on
the constant disappearing
translating
one measurement
into another

# WHEN THEY HAVE SENSES

*The Senses Barely,*
*or The Necessities of Life*

*for Sophie Hawkes*

I *(Weapons)*

doubled corners
of the situation

the words duped by this dialectic
know
the pose of "brushing against"

insistence
            on detail

severe eyelashes

        the weapons must
        be kept in order

        (take the
        game
        of courtesy
        of charm)

her knees crossed
over the manner of
his undressing her

a chord
                    (deceptively resonant)
a strength of image
but scanty provisions interrupt
her concern for doors


into sleep
focuses
the story can be carried in two hands


            finale:
                        I have turned on
                        with shifting strands
                        of light

II *(Pursuit)*

"I have turned on,
with sifting hands,
the light"

which in rehearsal
of place


he (I fear) resorts to trapping


or sits where atmosphere
exhausts the drifting ice
and the other inconsistencies


sits still in the slant
lays in stores
her skin
the bare necessities of life


(blurred crash
picks up a chair
a flash bulb stays
the position of the group)


distance
follows the slow argument
the pursuit of game
held back by the sleeve
untangled
a statue of Washington
          of songs

of burdens
of

cannibal spirits
do violence to words

III *(The Closing)*

they have no street in their hurry
but leave with the cold
and few household goods

                a body of pure salt
                stationary abode

preceded
by repetition
by empty bottles

the time it takes
to mix
the male and female
matter

none of the steps may be
omitted

                changes into
                unrecognizable
                straight lines

                    "she was with him"
                    the day after
                    in relative order
                    whereas

        the necessary eye
        of the sun
        overgrows

*The Senses Wolgamotly,*
*or There Were Men and Women*


I *(His Initiative)*

duped by the curve
the living tickle of revenge
of which a geometric cunning


                    changes wives


institutes trouble
the angle or how to
avoid it


I picked up and


                to which
            curiosity did
            he sell her
            now that secrecy seems
            irresistible


the crawling street
curb lined with bicycles
                experience (hive)
determines the doubt of the visit
the pleasure whose
repetition also
humiliates

smell of food
the execution
believed liquid


perplexed

## II *(His Method)*

whose humiliation he had
witnessed


he throws himself
into the law, the book, and thus
attracted
he figures a supple equation
in the eyes of his mistress


fake wishes (possible?)


responsible to circumstance
owed, that is, the
juridical paradox


                         sliced
her appeal deepens in his eyes

III *(Retrospective)*

this rehearsal is also
in the attitude

                      the fragrance of it
choked me
which cautions against contraries


the roles
that of the nape

                  in his first wife
                  her melancholy breath


generous, our haste,
my knees

                     do I lose the common torment
                     does he turn
                     whose manner to living

which
takes old conceptions like
"horses stiffened with priapic fury"


        for me
this is betrayal
or homage

IV *(His Greed)*

       food
reconciles his frame


he put my thumb in my mouth
or his, perhaps, supple
               so many jaws


pretends
because he can't cut the corner
of the mere thought of a meal


hefty
and only usual

# NOTHING HAS CHANGED

A sort of empty number
relations
never more present
all you
around you
let yourself
it moves but that's my fault
yes yes you said across the words

———

When did you
what a funny
he didn't anywhere
that is he lived and before
he found then why with you
he seemed and he
could stand the center of
to his surprise
more than she ever
awakened a distance with

———

The pressure not to live in
but streets and incessant
we're not
not really
would we accept
alone
to be not altogether

Parallel open so we could
against one another
turn
you know there is
between attention
a place never direct
nor an object to stay near
impersonal attention you don't with
extreme

———

Latent agreement not to
but suddenly we've been
always
movement toward presence
a secret
turns away
calmly

———

Give back what disappers
as if a detour in forgetting
could

# DIFFERENCES FOR FOUR HANDS

*for Michael Gizzi,*
*his part in it*

I

## CLARA & ROBERT SCHUMANN,
## AN INTRODUCTION

CLARA, I NEED TO TALK TO YOU. These keys are slippery. Fame tips your fingers. Between them, staves run out of brief happiness into the cold. Run. Seven children through the house. The Rhine into the sea.

Robert. Alarming symptoms, increasing frequency, A all around him, fear of death, shivering fits. Plunges: A-major into the river, and motion is stillness, the banks of the Rhine begin to flow along the water's stanched melody.

Clara, play for us. The performance over, your name drops back out of the air. Records now, of course. Groove dreams whipped stiff. You never stepped twice. Mortal moments, climate of blood. A fire that could melt our souls, but shades, gently, into the shapeless sea.

## II

## CLARA & ROBERT,
## A COURTSHIP

CLARA AND ROBERT, two rare talents, here in daguerreotype, smiling, a moment fixed between squalls of music.

Clara, the name looks good on a poster, announces, excessively thin, the six-year-old pianist, but "with more strength than six boys."

Clara in the "chiroplast" (for proper posture). Clara walking three hours a day (accompaniment: trees) "to get her nerves solid."

Robert in love, and time presses: "All of fourteen she is, skipping and running about like a child."
...

Green, green grass, all of fourteen and skipping and wild. But Robert fords rivers of coffins. Wind whips his eyes. A brother is not immortal, a mother not to take with you, lodged in the spine. Only the piano can vary the pitch of bruised eyelids, pit color against pain, rainbows in tenuous air. In this lies comfort. Solid slabs of sleep. Yet he wishes to be out of place. Already we see distress, extreme pulsating rushes of water.

Clara is famous and on tour.

"Clara, Clara, I'll put my chords in order. I'm clear about my heart, moody and restless, broken, violent, improbable and proven. It's impossible: Your father cannot refuse. I have complete confidence in my music and presentiments of death. I cannot stand in the wind. I'm more like venetian blinds than either heat or cold. Yet, though you say you love me, you go on tour with your father."

Cholera in Paris, recital washed out into hollow caution. But Vienna, Clara, there you turn pages. Of history, the "Appassionata," desires, whose and for what, Father Wieck's, his cloven hoof, his greed. Robert offended by absence.

Blows you the prick of a pen found on Beethoven's grave, rusty seal on a dream of waters stranger than deeper bodies to come. Metallic sighs, you know it gets lonely holding a pen, not a common rusty prayer. Cadence continues into color. Completed by an introspective slowness neither simple nor soft. Robert goes to court, minor key and cause.

Clara, your fingers drift, parallel fish, through preludes and fugues. There's time, you think, each drop a cool, nude promise. It's terribly time for Robert, for shortcuts to master technique: a fine contrivance, mechanical, sling up the fourth finger, straitjacket, the weak held straight and still and will never again move a key.

He is all clouds and shadow. Vacillates when he stops to think. Threatened by rivers. His quest for agitation sidetracks, restless eddies, fluid of eyes. He'd like to be still.

Clara give up something by marrying? Never occurs to him. Or her.

Any two are opposite. You walk on sound. The coldest wind blows from the edges of fear. Which has been written down. Passion's not natural. But body and soul are bruised by melancholy, fruit of dry, twisted riverbeds. Loss discolors the skin. At times you devour apples, at others bite into your hand.

III

CLARA & ROBERT,
A MARRIAGE

INTO HAPPINESS, into the *Well-Tempered Clavier*, Robert, perhaps
his two souls alas, his wayward moods, now into *Du meine Seele,* all
around him, a celebration for voice.

Form is defined as fits the years. Yet to stretch against softening: "frag-
ments, aphorisms, sheer reveling in strangeness." Plunge, head-on, into
his fears. Overlapping keys: the large tune, the constant, could be lost
in assuming endings. Golden light, not a blank which lies to your wor-
ries, a splendid body to body, relations of like and surprise worthy of
being desired.
...

And Clara. Cool and green, your moments, hammered in light. Love un-
der your skin. New color of keys. The very morning strokes you, a secret
music, before scales start running, and children's feet.

Clara on music: Not for a tickle of ears. I feel more clearly intimate. Ex-
pecting is a twofold breath, a second voice enters, subterranean stream.
More elements compressed into relation, in smaller circles. There are
only two sins: denying the sound, denying the silence. Together they let
the soul move through its inner space.

But many times impatient to practice: "Music's my vice, my secret plea-
sure and detachment." Thin walls, the evil of. Confluence of sounds.
Packed into the same dream, envy and desire: to carve into air too deep
for our errors. A static stream.

By what authority, wistful, her eyes on her piano, composer comes be-
fore pianist, husband before wife, and babies, babies. Run. Three chil-
dren through the house. Rename the dimensions Marie, Elise, Julie,
tune cut, repeated, turned in and out, voice close to sleep.

A complex grid, the fields of love, the way your mother bore you in the streets of Leipzig, the way Robert's skin stretches into your body, name wrapped in flesh. Wet rush. The land green and pregnant again.

"What will become of my work? But Robert says children are blessings."

Your body all around him.

Technique and passion, intelligence, grace. Dissonance rendered as dissonance, fire unfolding, electric. Much for your eye on meaning your body blazes the full force of the score, whirls our vertigo wide.
. . .

Run. Three children through the house. "What will become of my work?" Robert says procreation is music, a measure stolen on shivers, on fear of death.

Children all around him.

Into travels. You hold your head up. Pianist and wife. "I wish you would interpret my feelings a little more generously, accenting warmth which I mean central. I also owe it to my reputation not to retire completely. I shall be quite forgotten in a few years when perhaps we shall *want* to make a tour."

Robert would like to be still.

Clara, you won't be forgiven. Your secret pleasure and detachment. Cheeks flush, you mount the platform, ride his floundering storms.
"Companion to Clara."
"The artist's husband."
"Ah, Herr Schumann. Are you also a lover of music?"
. . .

IV

CLARA SUGGESTS AN APPOINTMENT

COULD HE NOT lift a baton, he had studied, not stand on a podium, with compositions his own and a wife and children?
...

Asymmetry is incurable. Sometimes understanding comes late. Image under eyelid. Rhythmic spasm. Expansion more diffident by means of an additional slow movement. All tempi are too fast. Compressed, melodic, large scale from minimal motive which is a bannister for all four movements to go safely without fear of falling, death, or violent shivers.

Run. Four children through the house.

Clara too confident, too hopeful, too black and white, because the piano. Runs. Clara. Her life, competently, hers, his, menaced and melancholy. Alarming symptoms, increasing frequency, 440 hertz, A all around him, cold wind at his heels, he marries the river.
...

The length of time Robert stands silent, common in solitary men, but judged unsuitable in a conductor: to take half an hour to bring down the baton? Unable to explain the note in his head, the waiting river, the reason, the parts to correct, the silence insistent. Didn't notice the strings had stopped, the choir left.

Run. Five children through the house.
...

In the grip of this theme, in the grip of fear. Bold repetition toward stillness, dangerous, with more than the usual figment. Full circle. All roads lead to A. Alarming symptoms, shivering fits, A in his ears, A all around him, aching orchestration and horror of arpeggios.

Clara plays. Her touch contains impossible *alternativos.* Containing is melancholy, but what other safeguard? Clara, play. Your belly swollen. Already late all around him. The theme enters in poignant nakedness, a momentary illumination, while embroidering sequence with gratitude and not abandoning, not ever abandoning a single note.

Run. Five children through the house.

"The noise of the carnival night changes into silence. The tower clock strikes six." Vertical sevenths fade along the river. He walks with a different voice now. Without preparation. Pushes to perplexity the change of tempo to wash off the sharp glandular stench. Abrupt all around him. Plunges, A-major, into the Rhine. All tempi are too fast, all notes A, all keys Clara's.

...

V

## WHEN A TRILL IS NOT FOLLOWED BY ANY NOTE, AT THE END, FOR INSTANCE, UNDERSTANDING IS LEFT TO ITSELF

DISSONANT CHORDS, exhausted with apprehension, Robert fished out of his Symphony by boatmen, each day of his death blue under your skin.
...

Jealous, Clara? He tossed himself first, the first stone. All madmen are beautiful. His body, naked amulet washed bland. You have no choice now. Run. Six children through the house. No giving in to shivers that strike the keys from your hand. You can't afford to give up ship. To sink into depression is a long blue that must be stopped. Can you stop it?

To ward off epidemics the college of physicians approves the firing of guns. A pianist's touch a personal matter, intangible. Too deeply earnest your eyes (blue). Your contrast between reality and difference, between grief. He of your love. Enter the only way your body. Love a matter of white cells. How long can you stand on your fingertips? His lips come to you out of a bandage of fog. You owe him. Another child, another stranger. Six children, not enough, not enough to drown the note in his brain all around him.

Clara. A schedule of constant travel. Six children want dinner. Keys plough the air. Clara, devoted, one of our finest, desperately holds on to the keys slip through her fingers, the works of Robert Schumann nearly drowned, a wound lodged under her skin. Clara, your sorrow, you hold it in, impossible *alternativo*, dig into the keyboard, touch gone to pain.
...

Run. Seven children through the house, seven children afraid of thunder, seven children in bed with the measles, one in his grave. And Robert. A white cell. Silence mounts to the ceiling, gelatinous waves.
...

A degree of impartiality, an intensity you demand of performance and give. Rip him whole from silence according to your art, a priestess. "You would hardly believe how the reverence for Robert is increasing. I cannot help feeling sad when it was here he made so many vain attempts."
. . .

"Ever since May the process of recovery has been arrested."

Plunged into his fear, the promise of bottom. Now the dark wave has folded over him and the heavenly music. A dead man's skin all around him.

Each day of his death. Nothing to hold but by a lame finger, immobile, still, a storm in the staves, tricks played by a postcard of pleasure. Not clarified by slipping into the river, his *Rhenish* Symphony. He can't be fished.

"I have pissed myself into the Rhine like a nightingale in vain washed into a fear of time. I confess its music is lovelier than my almost, almost, like breathing into your blue water. I hold I sang myself into a deep thirst, endless, like desire."

Clara, you won't be forgiven. Surviving. And by how long. Too practical, too competent. Not yours, the seal of pathos. Clara, I need to talk to you. I too admire the gift for destruction. I need your help on the long way round to death. Difficult. For all but the most sure-footed. You hold the keys, navigate the narrows, the space of music in the proportions of blood and air. Strongly the chords, the cascades of angels, falling in counterpoint and entire conclusion.

Play for us, Clara. Play the music we breathe.

*Differences for Four Hands* uses Lyn Hejinian's *Gesualdo* as a syntactical matrix. A direct quote from the book has been appropriated for Robert Schumann's voice.

# STREETS ENOUGH TO WELCOME SNOW

*Kind Regards*

*for & from Barbara Guest & Douglas Oliver*

1. *Kind Regards*

Your air of kind regards
kind randomness
of a museum
canvas sneakers
along with raspberry lips

*

lately you say I've had an awkward
pull
toward the past tense
my remarks renovate
details in oil

*

pantoufles all over again
in the slippery something that
should be your mind
does it matter about heels

## 2. *Silent as a Clam*

yesterday I saw a word
stopped
in the breath its
natural home

\*

mouthy dreams with fishing
lines attached
such fierce hope in a hook
night crawls on
so spooky in a German fashion
I picture it
deepening into
a body of water

\*

confused terrain and pubic
hair a movement
of its own the
shuddering air

## 3. *Salt*

the house accepts me tentatively
grey
saltbeaten
and relaxed sand
drags across the floor but its
stomach muscles stretching toward
the tide line green sheet
draws back
taking its image
a few gulls flung for direction

*

the instant stretches into lateness
and onions
spoil the effect

not a perfect day

*

I admire your worrying away
(in your own phrase)
at sentences    I also like
the porchlamp fishing rod
even the baby its bundle of blankets
but especially that wink always back
of your words
nearly avoiding exact reference

## 4. *Correspondence*

the piano chooses conspiracy
the way it seals the room
(and you pulling his beard all the while)
like a ship torpedoed those
sounds too large and shiny
step suddenly
into a different time-scale

distance
quiet water

*

easy equations like chords of sunlight
or the color blindness of one pursued
by after-images

*

clearly more serious
by correspondence
without the
groceries of sociability

## 5. *No Hurry to Struggle*

a sore throat and memories
the moment clings

*

even though a swarm of light
behind your lids
self-firing
neurons
a little energy goes a long
residue
Dutch oven
still
the lid can't hold the "flavor of eyes"

*

at first kind
(regards) then comfortable stratagems
now only our tension left
above water
before you disconnect the ripples and dizziness
pulse fastened
lucidly
on my left retina

whistles across wave-tops

## 6. *Drawbridge*

missing premonitions in the
afternoon I stuff
the air with errors and
revise my walks
because of the glass door

I welcome your visits

*

we talk as long as we can
there are amazements
you like to stray into and
my body's only
one of them

*

rubbing against the outside
to avoid as best I can
the steep slope inward
I like the shreds of scenery
I can carry into the lamp-light
hesitant shrubs like a tentative
loss of memory in its
silvery green
a drawbridge

## 7. *So Long*

butterflies
distort every mention of sand
you punctuate your feelings
with a puff
on your pipe
a thing or two will come up
around the edges
you can guess
the effort behind a red cloud

\*

the house comes crowding round
to seduce us with
not quite oriental rugs

\*

irrelevant patches
light mostly
elsewhere a joke and then
the white blouse
more sun and the girl selling ice cream
there on the beach
skirt caught
the wind
hugging its visibility

*Psyche & Eros*

for Harriet Hanger & Peter Craske

I. *The Marriage*

For all her beauty
worshipped
but unloved

what greater complaint
when the damp towels
curl up
in baby form

abrupt sense of home life

but marriage is certain

I believe
the girl *wants* to die

maturing
caught on a back stroke

finger language

she must have lain
down in a place of caves
as if wet earth
a resting place for blood

        for the dark
        swoop
        strokes her body
        into bird

## II. *The Crisis*

That she should suffer
from happiness
its ambiguity
neither watching the time
nor making it contagious

the sisters: breaking the
blinds
punch waves of dust
and rainy fear
at any rate: they
cheerfull step on the brake

"it isn't for taking
your pulse
       (its panicky skid)
but a serious addition to knowledge"

| | |
|---|---|
| so she says she can't | that's right |
| live | (say the sisters) |
| being in the | a foul |
| dark | venemous |
| sweet | snake |
| honey | with tangled coils exuding |
| eyes tucked in under | darkness |
| feathered lids that no | it rears |
| square of skin should escape | up for |
| his caress | you even |
| | now |

in short:
      drowned
in a slick of pleasure

III. *The Catastrophy*

Not so dreadful, really, what
she does:

opens
more than her legs

                    but he
                    can't take it
                    this eye to
                    eye encounter
                    when what he wants is a lay

                    the lamp scalds him the light
                    enlarges
                    his notion of hurt

                    the burn
                    and the bandage both
                    making memory

          the earth doesn't
          turn
          it's deflected

          it's his back
          turns

          he walks off
          the same

IV. *The Labors*

So it comes to this
(always?)

direction: labor
to get him
back
get him to

           corn barley millet poppy
           chickpeas lentils
           beans in a heap all the
           seeds in a heap the
           seeds of the world a
           promiscuous heap

           and they laugh at her:
           chaos is human what more
           do you want

love you
as separate
a person

        what woman dreams light
        must face the sun
        dreams fierce and blinding
        dreams waiting for evening
        dreams golden rams
        a vestige of sun
        you can love and live

but life
the river   who could
contain it

           stream of semen
           in a hip flask

and the last and hardest:
the trip
down
where
the blood
slows
her feet are
dragging
they
won't they won't lift

no horses
whinny
        she breathes
sleep     it's a journey
to death

it would keep her beauty forever

answer: she's tempted
(to please her lover)

                    But he
                        a taste
                        of the past tense
                        has stretched his
                        one way grammar

                        now
                        he'll rather have her
                        grow old

                    and comes to her aid

             a happy ending: to love
             love knowingly
             body and soul

in the old story
they call it going
to heaven

from *The Ambition of Ghosts*


*Home Drown*

1.


Bach on Sundays, again, in
so many churches. The
synagogue
a ruin. Also Gedächtniskirche.
Some chords, still, between scorched
arches, hold
my breath
                    though the air,
here,
is sealed
against seepage.
                    What
was it, mother.
More wishes
on the bone. Gold,
articulated
bars, warm, in your throat.
Or hand.
                    Baroque,
the space between
words and
what has "happened."
                    Like, in 1749,
the Prinz von Anhalt
was struck by *fascination*
and "couldn't
see anything as
it was."
                    Your steel's
caved in, mother, its
blue sheen
drowned.

2.

A place repeated
inhales
time
seeps through
the layers of years.
Enlarged river bed, eroded,
this,
my porous skin.
                    Half
of Pascal's body
was glass. He always saw,
on that side, the abyss.
Crystal
nights.
                If I
were sure I'm drowning. If
I could solve
my memories. They gather
to eat. But I've unlearned
pity. Mother,
always a little colder,
floats
among the algae, eyes
beginning to rust.


3. TELL ME ABOUT YOUR ILLNESS, MOTHER

"I'm so planned. And nearly
crying. No, no, I'm song, the smell of scales
doesn't upset a widow.
But streets, their bubbles:
suddenly
the fish inside my head. Just
when I kneel
down on the curb to play

for my lost
keys.
*You* are unnaturally tall,
I nearly couldn't seal you. We'll
have to
grind
your parts into the score.
And now good night, my chill,
it's time
to climb into my wishes."


4.

This is where hands clutch at
a door, straw, wisp of smoke
pulls out my breath.
My eyes,
all my eyes tremble and
run from my head in long flight.
Be calm. Don't forget.
Go tap the dark for unsuspected
switches, a way
out of this, the furniture,
its cold sheen,
to what? The furious
grief springs on your back, ardent
reproach, a reddish seal.
"O thunderweather," swears Old Shatterhand. How
like frightened, trying
to relax his smallness
into the wild space of the West such as,
but this,
this anguish, think of seeing:
your mother
turned liquid.
Grey wash, warm, on the floor.

## 5. NIGHTMARE

Farther and farther
off key, this,
warm air, even
breathing. Mother
peals the skin back,
and a red sheen breaks,
sears
my lungs. I can't
swim
against the dream.
Only a tight
layer of perfect pitch
could seal
my bloodstream against

                      Next
scene. The river,
present, and full up. Still,
bubbles from
deep years, and mother
pulls out a plaster cunt:

                        "This is
your flesh."
              The air
bursts with drowned fish
If I could solve my
memories
              would I
awake?

## 6. LEAVING

"Only drowned souls
can't
come back to haunt you
in the channels
of your body, a fire
goes out
in water."
                  Old selves
seep through my
skin, no tenderness
in our mutual muscles.
                              Distance,
growing, drifts
between our words, the air
hard with motion,
even a song
can turn into a demon:
warm air, even
breathing, living, articulated
limbs,
and the window rattling
the whole time.
                        Try
to keep an eye
on your tears,
mother,
you've never
gone near water but to drown.

# THE REPRODUCTION OF PROFILES

*Facts*

I HAD INFERRED from pictures that the world was real and therefore paused, for who knows what will happen if we talk truth while climbing the stairs. In fact, I was afraid of following the picture to where it reaches right out into reality, laid against it like a ruler. I thought I would die if my name didn't touch me, or only with its very end, leaving the inside open to so many feelers like chance rain pouring down from the clouds. You laughed and told everybody that I had mistaken the Tower of Babel for Noah in his Drunkenness.

I DIDN'T WANT to take this street which would lead me back home, by my own cold hand, or your advice to find some other man to hold me because studying one headache would not solve the problem of sensation. All this time, I was trying to think, but the river and the bank fused into common darkness, and words took on meanings that made them hard to use in daylight. I believed entropy meant hugging my legs close to my body so that the shadow of the bridge over the Seekonk could be written into the hub of its abandoned swivel.

THE PROPORTION OF ACCIDENT in my picture of the world falls with the rain. Sometimes, at night, diluted air. You told me that the poorer houses down by the river still mark the level of the flood, but the world divides into facts like surprised wanderers disheveled by a sudden wind. When you stopped preparing quotes from the ancient misogynists it was clear that you would soon forget my street.

I HAD ALREADY STUDIED mathematics, a mad kind of horizontal reasoning like a landscape that exists entirely on its own, when it is more natural to lie in the grass and make love, glistening, the whole length of the river. Because small, noisy waves, as from strenuous walking, pounded in my ears, I stopped my bleak Saturday, while a great many dry leaves dropped from the sycamore. This possibility must have been in color from the beginning.

FLOODING WITH IMPULSE refracts the body and does not equal. Duck wings opened, jeweled, ablaze in oblique flight. Though a speck in the visual field must have some color, it need not be red. Or beautiful. A mountain throwing its shadow over so much nakedness, or a cloud lighting its edges on the sun, it drowned my breath more deeply, and things lost their simple lines to possibility. Like old idols, you said, which we no longer adore and throw into the current to drift where they still

## Feverish Propositions

YOU TOLD ME, if something is not used it is meaningless, and took my temperature, which I had thought to save for a more difficult day. In the mirror, every night, the same face, a bit more threadbare, a dress worn too long. The moon was out in the cold, along with the restless, dissatisfied wind that seemed to change the location of the sycamores. I expected reproaches because I had mentioned the word love, but you only accused me of stealing your pencil, and sadness disappeared with sense. You made a ceremony out of holding your head in your hands because, you said, it could not be contained in itself.

IF WE COULD JUST go on walking through these woods and let the pine branches brush our faces, living would still make beads of sweat on your forehead, but you wouldn't have to worry about what you call my exhibitionism. All you liked about trees was the way the light came through the leaves in sheets of precise, parallel rays, like slant rain. This may be an incomplete explanation of our relation, but we've always feared the dark inside the body. You agree there could be no seduction if the structures of propositions did not stand in a physical relation, so that we could get from one to the other. Even so, not every moment of happiness is to hang one's clothes on.

I MIGHT HAVE KNOWN you wouldn't talk to me. But to claim you just didn't want to disguise your thoughts! We've walked along this road before, I said, though perhaps in heavier coats not designed to reveal the form of the body. Later, the moon came out and threw the shadows of branches across the street where they remained, broken. Feverishly you examined the tacit conventions on which conversation depends. I sighed as one does at night, looking down into the river. I wondered if by throwing myself in I could penetrate to the essence of its character, or should I wait for you to stab me as you had practiced in your dream? You said this question, like most philsophical problems, arose from failing to understand the tale of the two youths, two horses, and two lilies. You could prove to me that the deepest rivers are, in fact, no rivers at all.

FROM THIS OBSERVATION we turned to consider passion. Looking at the glints of light on the water, you tried to make me tell you not to risk the excitement—to recommend cold baths. The lack of certainty, of direction, of duration, was its own argument, unlike going into a bar to get drunk and getting drunk. Your face was alternately hot and cold, as if translating one language into another—gusts from the storm in your heart, the pink ribbon in your pocket. Its actual color turned out to be unimportant, but its presence disclosed something essential about membranes. You said there was still time, you could still break it off, go abroad, make a movie. I said (politely, I thought) this wouldn't help you. You'd have to kill yourself.

TEARING YOUR SHIRT OPEN, you drew my attention to three dogs in a knot. This served to show how something general can be recorded in unpedigreed notation. I pointed to a bench by a willow, from which we could see the gas tanks across the river, because I thought a bench was a simple possibility: one could sit on it. The black hulks of the tanks began to sharpen in the cold dawn light, though when you leaned against the railing I could smell your hair, which ended in a clean round line on your neck, as was the fashion that year. I had always resented how nimble your neck became whenever you met a woman, regardless of rain falling outside or other calamities. Now, at least, you hunched your shoulders against the shadow of doubt.

THIS TIME OF DAY, hesitation can mean tottering on the edge, just before the water breaks into the steep rush and spray of the fall. What could I do but turn with the current and get choked by my inner speed? You tried to breathe against the acceleration, waiting for the air to consent. All the while, we behaved as if this search for a pace were useful, like reaching for a plank or wearing rain coats. I was afraid we would die before we could make a statement, but you said that language presupposed meaning, which would be swallowed by the roar of the waterfall.

TOWARD MORNING, WALKING along the river, you tossed simple objects into the air which was indifferent around us, though it moved off a little, and again as you put your hand back in your pocket to test the degree of hardness. Everything else remained the same. This is why, you said, there was no fiction.

from *Inserting the Mirror*

TO EXPLORE THE NATURE of rain I opened the door because inside the workings of language clear vision is impossible. You think you see, but are only running your finger through pubic hair. The rain was heavy enough to fall into this narrow street and pull shreds of cloud down with it. I expected the drops to strike my skin like a keyboard. But I only got wet. When there is no resonance, are you more likely to catch a cold? Maybe it was the uniform appearance of the drops which made their application to philosophy so difficult even though the street was full of reflection. In the same way, fainting can, as it approaches, slow the Yankee Doodle to a near loss of pitch. I watched the outline of the tower grow dim until it was only a word in my brain. That language can suggest a body where there is none. Or does a body always contain its own absecnce? The rain, I thought, ought to protect me against such arid speculations.

THE BODY IS USEFUL. I can send it on errands while I stay in bed and pull the blue blanket up to my neck. Once I coaxed it to get married. It trembled and cried on the way to the altar, but then gently pushed the groom down to the floor and sat on him while the family crowded closer to get in on the excitement. The black and white flagstones seemed to be rocking, though more slowly than people could see, which made their gestures uncertain. Many of them slipped and lay down. Because they closed their eyes in the hope of opening their bodies I rekindled the attentions of love. High-tension wires very different from propensity and yet again from mirror images. Even if we could not remember the color of heat the dominant fuel would still consume us.

I LEARNED ABOUT COMMUNICATION by twisting my legs around yours as, in spinning a thought, we twist fiber on fiber. The strength of language does not reside in the fact that some one desire runs its whole length, but in the overlapping of many generations. Relationships form before they are written down just as grass bends before the wind, and now it is impossible to know which of us went toward the other, naked, unsteady, but, once lit, the unprepared fused with its afterimage like twenty stories of glass and steel on fire. Our lord of the mirror. I closed my eyes afraid to resemble.

IS IT POSSIBLE to know where a word ends and my use of it begins? Or to locate the ledge of your promises to lean my head on? Even if I built a boundary out of five pounds of definition it could not be called the shock of a wall. Nor the pain that follows. Dusk cast the houses in shadow, flattening their projections. Blurred edges, like memory or soul, an event you turn away from. Yet I also believe that a sharp picture is not always preferable. Even when people come in pairs, their private odds should be made the most of. You went in search of more restful altitudes, of ideally clear language. But the bridge that spans the mind-body gap enjoys gazing downstream. All this time I was holding my umbrella open.

# LAWN OF EXCLUDED MIDDLE

from *Lawn of Excluded Middle*

WHEN I SAY I believe that women have a soul and that its substance contains two carbon rings the picture in the foreground makes it difficult to find its application back where the corridors get lost in ritual sacrifice and hidden bleeding. But the four points of the compass are equal on the lawn of the excluded middle where full maturity of meaning takes time the way you eat a fish, morsel by morsel, off the bone. Something that can be held in the mouth, deeply, like darkness by someone blind or the empty space I place at the center of each poem to allow penetration.

I PUT A RULER in my handbag, having heard men talk about their sex. Now we have correct measurements and a stickiness between collar and neck. It is one thing to insert yourself into a mirror, but quite another to get your image out again and have your errors pass for objectivity. Vitreous. As in humor. A change in perspective is caused by the ciliary muscle, but need not be conciliatory. Still, the eye is a camera, room for everything that is to enter, like the cylinder called the satisfaction of hollow space. Only language grows such grass-green grass.

BECAUSE I REFUSE to accept the opposition of night and day I must pit other, subtler periodicities against the emptiness of being an adult. Their traces inside my body attempt precariously, like any sign, to produce understanding, but though nothing may come of that, the grass is growing. Can words play my parts and also find their own way to the house next door as rays converge and solve their differences? Or do notes follow because drawn to a conclusion? If we don't signal our love, reason will eat our heart out before it can admit its form of mere intention, and we won't know what has departed.

IT'S A TALL ORDER that expects pain to crystallize into beauty. And we must close our eyes to conceive of heaven. The inside of the lid is fertile in images unprovoked by experience, or perhaps its pressure on the eyeball equals prayer in the same way that inference is a transition toward assertion, even observing rites of dawn against a dark and empty background. I have read that female prisoners to be hanged must wear rubber pants and a dress sewn shut around the knees because uterus and ovaries spill with the shock down the shaft.


I WORRIED ABOUT THE GAP between expression and intent, afraid the world might see a fluorescent advertisement where I meant to show a face. Sincerity is no help once we admit to the lies we tell on nocturnal occasions, even in the solitude of our own heart, wishcraft slanting the naked figure from need to seduce to fear of possession. Far better to cultivate the gap itself with its high grass for privacy and reference gone astray. Never mind that it is not philosophy, but raw electrons jumping from orbit to orbit to ready the pit for the orchestra, scrap meanings amplifying the succession of green perspectives, moist features, spasms on the lips.


IN PROVIDENCE, you can encounter extinct species, an equestrian statue, say, left hoof raised in progress toward the memory of tourists. Caught in its career of immobility, but with surface intact, waiting to prove that it can resist the attack of eyes even though dampened by real weather, even though historical atmosphere is mixed with exhaust, like etymology with the use of a word, or bone with sentence structure. No wonder we find it difficult to know our way about and tend to stay indoors.

THIS IS NOT THINKING, you said, more what colors it, like a smell entering our breath even to the seat of faith under the left nipple. Like the children I could have borne shaping my body toward submission and subterfuge. It is possible, I admitted, to do physics in inches as well as in centimeters, but a concept is more than a convenience. It takes us through earnest doorways to always the same kind of example. No chance of denser vegetation, of the cool shadow of firs extending this line of reasoning into the dark.

MY LOVE WAS DEEP and therefore lasted only the space of one second, unable to expand in more than one dimension at a time. The same way deeper meaning may constrict a sentence right out of the language into an uneasiness with lakes and ponds. In language nothing is hidden or our own, its light indifferent to holes in the present or postulates beginning with ourselves. Still, you may travel alone and yet be accompanied by my good wishes.

I WANTED TO SETTLE down on a surface, a map perhaps, where my near-sightedness might help me see the facts. But grammar is deep. Even though it only describes, it submerges the mind in a maelstrom without discernible bottom, the dimensions of possibles swirling over the fixed edge of nothingness. Like looking into blue eyes all the way through to the blue sky without even a cloudbank or flock of birds to cling to. What are we searching behind the words as if a body of information could not also bruise? It is the skeleton that holds on longest to its native land.

YOU WERE DETERMINED to get rid of your soul by expressing it completely, rubbing the silver off the mirror in hope of a new innocence of body on the other side of knowing. A limpid zone which would not wholly depend on our grammar in the way the sea draws its color from the sky. Noon light, harsh, without shadow. Each gesture intending only its involvement with gravity, a pure figure of reach, as the hyperbola is for its asymptotes or circles widening on the water for the stone that broke the surface. But the emigration is rallied, reflections regather across the ripples. Everything in our universe curves back to the apple.

AS IF I HAD to navigate both forward and backward, part of me turned away from where I'm going, taking the distance of long corridors to allow for delay and trouble, for keeping in the dark while being led on. In this way Chinese characters seem to offer their secret without revealing it, invitation to enter a labyrinth which, like that of the heart, may not have a center. It is replaced by being lost which I don't like to dwell on because the search for motivation can only drive us downward toward potential that is frightening in proportion to its depth and sluicegates to disappearance. It is much better, I have been advised, just to drift with the stream. The ink washes into a deeper language, and in the end the water runs clear.

from *The Perplexing Habit of Falling*

IN THE BEGINNING there were torrential rains, and the world dissolved in puddles, even though we were well into the nuclear age and speedier methods. Constant precipitation drenched the dry point of the present till it leaked a wash of color all the way up to the roots of our hair. I wanted to see mysteries at the bottom of the puddles, but they turned out to be reflections that made our heads swim. The way a statue's eyes bring our stock of blindness to the surface. Every thought swelled to the softness of flesh after a long bath, the lack of definition essential for happiness, just as not knowing yourself guarantees a life of long lukewarm days stretching beyond the shadow of pure reason on the sidewalk. All this was common practice. Downpour of sun. Flood of young leafiness. A slight unease caused by sheer fill of body. Running over and over like the light spilled westward across the continent, a river we couldn't cross without our moment, barely born, drowning in its own translucent metaphor.

MY LEGS WERE SO interlaced with yours I began to think I could never use them on my own again. Not even if I shaved them. As if emotion had always to be a handicap. But maybe the knots were a picture of my faint unrest at having everything and not more, like wind caught in the trees with no open space to get lost, a tension toward song hanging in the air like an unfinished birdcry, or the smell of the word verbena, or apples that would not succumb to the attraction of the ground. In a neutral grammar love may be a refrain screamed through the loudspeakers, a calibration of parallels, or bone structure strong enough to support verisimilitude. A FOR SALE sign in red urged us to participate in our society, while a whole flock of gulls stood in the mud by the river, ready to extend the sky with their wings. Another picture. Is it called love or nerves, you said, when everything is on the verge of happening? But I was unable to distinguish between waves and corpuscles because I had rings under my eyes, and appearances are fragile. Though we already live partly underground it must be possible to find a light that is exacting and yet allows us to be ourselves even while taking our measure.

YOUR ARMS WERE EMBRACING like a climate that does not require being native. They held me responsive, but I still wondered about the other lives I might have lived, the unused cast of characters stored within me, outcasts of actuality no stranger than my previous selves. As if a word should be counted a lie for all it misses. I could imagine my body arching up toward other men in a high-strung vertigo that scored a virtual accompaniment to our real dance, deep phantom chords echoing from nowhere though with the force of long acceleration, of flying home from a lost wedding. Stakes and mistakes. Big with sky, with bracing cold, with the drone of aircraft, the measures of distance hang in the air before falling in thick drops. The child will be pale and thin. Though it had infiltrated my bones, the thought was without marrow. More a feeling that might accompany a thought, a ply of consonants, an outward motion of the eye.

MANY QUESTIONS were left in the clearing we built our shared life in. Later sheer size left no room for imagining myself standing outside it, on the edge of an empty day. I knew I didn't want to part from this whole which could be said to carry its foundation as much as resting on it, just as a family tree grows downward, its branches confounding gravitation and gravidity. I wanted to continue lying alongside you, two parallel, comparable lengths of feeling, and let the stresses of the structure push our sleep to momentum and fullness. Still, a fallow evening stretching into unknown elsewheres, seductive with possibility, doors open onto a chaos of culs-de-sac, of could-be, of galloping off on the horse in the picture. And whereto? A crowning mirage or a question like, What is love? And where? Does it enter with a squeeze, or without, bringing, like interpretation, its own space from some other dimension? Or is it like a dream corridor forever extending its concept toward extreme emptiness, like that of atoms?

EVEN AT YOUR NAKEDEST, your nakedness would not reach all the way to your face, the way a rock by the sea is always veiled in water and foam as in a memory of deep space. Or perhaps I was looking for something beyond my capacity of seeing, and the shifts of hiddenness were only in the image I carried somewhere between head and dark of stomach as I searched the woods for poisonous mushrooms. The technique is to knock them out with a stick and tread them to pulp which saves lives and provides entertainment. Actually I prefer stories with sharp edges cut by blades manufactured with great precision in Solingen, Germany. These I use like a religion to keep me on the straight and narrative which, like computers and gods, admits only yes or no. No straying into ambiguous underbrush where hidden desire is not made any clearer by intermittent fulfillment, the light and shadow playing over my rush of wildwater actions while I feel I'm sitting motionless on the bank.


WITH THE BODY running down inexorably, how can we each day reweave our net of closeness and distance? But though time burns at both ends, it rolls around the clock, and evening replays events of the day in a new light, showing perhaps electric waves instead of raindrops, glittering on a spiderweb. The relation is not resemblance, but pulling the trigger on a nerve. While time takes the shortest cut right into consciousness, physical cause stops at the door. There remains an ultimate gap, as between two people, that not even a penis can bridge, a point at which we lose sight of the erection crossing a horizon in the mind. This is accompanied by slight giddiness as when we jump over our shadow or admire the waves rolling incomprehensible resolutions in a border of darker and darker gray. It dispenses us from trying to draw profit from attention to ritual, like watching the spider ride its memory from periphery to center orb at nightfall.

I BADLY WANTED a story of my own. As if there were proof in spelling. But what if my experience were the kind of snow that does not accumulate? A piling of instants that did not amount to a dimension? What if wandering within my own limits I came back naked, with features too faint for the mirror, unequal to the demands of the night? In the long run I could not deceive appearances: Days and nights were added without adding up. Nothing to recount in bed before falling asleep. Even memory was not usable, a landscape hillocky with gravitation but without monuments, it did not hold the eye, did not hinder its glide toward the horizon where the prose of the world gives way to the smooth functioning of fear. If the wheel so barely touches the ground the speed must be enormous.

I KNEW that true or false is irrelevant in the pursuit of knowledge which must find its own ways to avoid falling as it moves toward horizons of light. We can't hope to prove gravity from the fact that it tallies with the fall of an apple when the nature of tallying is what Eve's bite called into question. My progress was slowed down by your hand brushing against my breast, just as travel along the optic nerve brakes the rush of light. But then light does not take place, not even in bed. It is like the kind of language that vanishes into communication, as you might into my desire for you. It takes attention focused on the fullness of shadow to give light a body that weighs on the horizon, though without denting its indifference.

I THOUGHT I COULD get to the bottom of things by taking my distance from logic, but only fell as far as the immediate. Here the moment flaunted its perfect roundness and could not be left behind because it accelerated with me, intense like roses blooming in the dark whereas I was still figuring out: are red roses at night darker than white ones, and all cats gray? But at some point we have to pass from explanation to description in the heroic hope that it will reach right out into experience, the groundswell flooding my whole being like heat or pollution, though the haze outside always looks as if it could easily be blown away. A cat of any color can descend into the pit behind her eyes and yawn herself right back to the bland surfaces that represent the world in the logical form we call reality. But logic is no help when you have no premises. And more and more people lacking the most modest form of them are wandering through the streets. Do we call the past perfect because it is out of sight? The present person singular is open to terrifying possibilities that strip off skin till I weep as when peeling onions.

FINALLY I CAME to prefer the risk of falling to the arrogance of solid ground and placed myself on the thin line of translation, balancing precariously between body harnessed to slowness and categories of electric charge whizzing across fields nobody could stand on. Working the charge against my retina into the cognate red of a geranium I wondered if the direction of translation should be into arithmetic or back into my native silence. Or was this a question like right or left, reversible? And could it be resolved on the nonstandard model of androgyny, sharing out the sensitive zones among the contenders? Meanwhile everyday language is using all its vigor to keep the apple in the habit of falling though the curve of the world no longer fits our flat feet and matter's become too porous to place them on.

# RELUCTANT GRAVITIES

*Prologue: Two Voices*

Two voices on a page. Or is it one? Now turning in on themselves, back into fiber and leaf, now branching into sequence, consequence, public works projects or discord. Now touching, now trapped in frames without dialog box. Both tentative, as if poring over old inscriptions, when perhaps the wall is crumbling, circuits broken, pages blown off by a fall draft.

Even if voices wrestle on the page, their impact on the air is part of their definition. In a play, for instance, the sentences would be explained by their placement on stage. We would not ask an actress what anguish her lines add up to. She would not worry what her voice touches, would let it spill over the audience, aiming beyond the folds of the curtain, at the point in the distance called the meaning of the play.

The difference of our sex, says one voice, saves us from humiliation. It makes me shiver, says the other. Your voice drops stones into feelings to sound their depth. Then warmth is truncated to war. But I'd like to fall back into simplicity as into a featherbed.

Voices, planted on the page, do not ripen or bear fruit. Here placement does not explain, but cultivates the vacancy between them. The voices pause, start over. Gap gardening which, moved inward from the right margin, suspends time. The suspension sets, is set, in type, in columns that precipitate false memories of garden, vineyard, trellis. Trembling leaf, rules of black thumb and white, invisible angle of breath and solid state.

She tries to draw a strength she dimly feels out of the weaknesses she knows, as if predicting an element in the periodic table. He wants to make a flat pebble skim across the water inside her body. He wonders if, for lack of sky, it takes on the color of skin or other cells it touches. If it rusts the bones.

The pact between page and voice is different from the compact of voice and body. The voice opens the body. Air, the cold of the air, passes through and, with a single inflection, builds large castles. The page wants proof, but bonds. The body cannot keep the voice. It spills. Foliage over the palisade.

He has put a pebble under his tongue. While her lips explode in conjectures his lisp is a new scale to practice. He wants his words to lift, against the added odds, to a truth outside him. In exchange, his father walking down the road should diminish into a symbol of age.

The page lures the voice with a promise of wood blossoming. But there is no air. No breath lives in the mouth or clouds the mirror. On stage, the body would carry the surface we call mind. Here, surface marries surface, refusing deep waters. Still, the point of encounter is here, always. Screams rise. Tears fall. Impure white, legible.

*Conversation 1*
*On the Horizontal*


My mother, she says, always spread, irresistibly, across the entire room, flooding me with familiarity to breed content. I feared my spongy nature and, hoping for other forms of absorption, opened the window onto more water, eyes level with its surface. And lower, till the words "I am here" lost their point with the vanishing air. Just as it's only in use that a proposition grinds its lens.

Deciphering, he says, is not a horizontal motion. Though the way a sentence is meant can be expressed by an expansion that becomes part of it. As a smile may wide-open a door. Holding the tools in my mouth I struggle uphill, my body so perfectly suspended between my father's push and gravity's pull that no progress is made. As if consciousness had to stay embedded in carbon. Or copy. Between camp and bomb. But if you try to sound feelings with words, the stone drops into reaches beyond fathoms.

I *am* here, she says, I've learned that life consists in fitting my body to the earth's slow rotation. So that the way I lean on the parapet betrays dried blood and invisible burns. My shadow lies in the same direction as all the others, and I can't jump over it. My mother's waves ran high. She rode them down on me as on a valley, hoping to flush out the minerals. But I hid my bones under sentences expanding like the flesh in my years.

Language, he says, spells those who love it, sliding sidelong from word to whole cloth. The way fingers extend the body into adventure, print, lakes, and Dead-man's-hand. Wherever the pen pushes, in the teeth of fear and malediction, even to your signature absorbing you into sign. A discomfort with the feel of home before it grows into inflamed tissue and real illness. With symptoms of grammar, punctuation, subtraction of soul. And only death to get you out.

*Conversation 2*
*On the Vertical*


We must decipher our lives, he says, forward and backward, down through cracks in the crystal to excrement, entrails, formation of cells. And up. The way the lark at the end of night trills vertically out of the grass—and even that I know too vaguely, so many blades and barely sharper for the passing of blindness—up into anemic heights, the stand-still of time. Could we call this God? or meaning?

The suck of symbol, rather, she quotes. Or an inflection of the voice? Let the song go on. And time. My shadow locks my presence to the ground. It's real enough and outside myself, though regularly consumed at high noon. So maybe I should grant the shoot-out: light may flood me too, completely. But it won't come walking in boots and spurs, or flowing robes, and take my hand or give me the finger with the assurance of a more rational being. And my body slopes toward yours no matter how level the ground.

If we can't call it God, he says, it still perches on the mind, minting strangeness. How could we recognize what we've never seen? A whale in through the window, frame scattered as far as non-standard candles. The sky faints along the giant outline, thar she blows under your skin, tense, a parable right through the body that remains so painfully flesh.

So pleasurably flesh, she says, and dwells among us, flesh offered to flesh, thick as thieves, beginning to see. Even the lark's soar breaks and is content to drop back into yesterday's gravity. Which wins out over dispersion, even doubt, and our thoughts turn dense like matter. The way the sky turns deep honey at noon. The way my sensations seem to belong to a me that has always already sided with the world.

*Conversation 3*
*On Vertigo*


That's why thought, he says, means fear. Sicklied o'er with the pale cast. And the feel of a woman. No boundary or edge. No foothold. Blast outspins gravity, breath to temples, gut to throat, propositions break into gasps. Then marriage. The projectile returns to the point of firing. Shaken, I try to take shelter in ratios of dots on a screen.

A narrow bed, she says. Easier to internalize combustion under a hood while rain falls in sheets, glazing a red wheelbarrow for the hell of it. I don't bait fabled beasts to rise to the surface of intonation. But I once watched a rooster mate, and he felt hard inside me, a clenched fist, an alien rock inside me, because there was no thinking to dissolve him. So to slide down, so unutterably, so indifferent.

I don't understand, he says, how manifest destiny blows west with the grass, how the word "soul" floats through the language the way pollen pervades tissue. Worry pivots in the gut, a screeching brake, so scant the difference between mistake and mental disturbance. Is language our cockadoodledoo? Is thinking a search for curves? Do I need arrowheads or dreadlocks to reach my rawest thoughts? A keyboard at their edge?

The longer I watched, she says, the more distinctly did I feel the snap of that shot flat inside me. So simple the economy of nature: space appears along with matter. So to slide down and stand there. Such self-gravity. So narrow the gap between mistake and morning sickness.

*Conversation 4*
*On Place*

I sit in my own shadow, she says, the way my mother gave birth to it. In artificial light, blinds drawn against the darkness of power. I think of you as if you were that shadow, a natural enclosure, a world, not a slight, so I can wander through your darkness. Has our contract inverted time, made our universe contract, a cramped bed for two? And when I say your name, do I draw water, a portrait, curtain, bridge, or conclusion?

Place there is none, he quotes. Not even to hang up our archetypes. Let alone Star Spangled Banners. We go forward and backward, and there is no place. Therefore it is a name for God. My eye, steadfast on traffic lights, abolishes the larger part of the round world. I should look at my feet. Space sweeps through us, a hell of distances bathed in the feeble glow of emptiness. Outward mobility, unimpeded. Suddenly we're nobody home, without any need of inattention, imposture, or talent for deceit.

The wind whips my skin as if it were water, she says. My skin *is* water. For wind read wind, news, sky falling. Is it a mental disturbance or the higher math of love if I hear you talking under my breath and from the torn fragments assume the sun is far away and small, and a look can cause a burn? Superstition, too, is a kind of understanding, and to forgo it may have consequences.

Clusters of possibilities whiz through our head, he says. Electric charges, clogged highway, screeching brakes, a house too full of guests. With grounds for disagreement and miscarriage. The light rushes in dry, screaming. But the opaque parts of the nerve oppose the noise and void the options. Then the project must be prolonged in terms of lack.

*Interlude*

*Song*

long
as in hypnosis
not easeful by half
in love

a white jug with flower
no room
among pictures
from within

look how even of dreams
we try to make sense

*Meditation on Fact*

"I know" is supposed to express a relation between me and a fact.

old arteries acquainted with

Where fact is taken into consciousness like your body into mine, and I'm all sponge and crevice, floating heat and sold but for the tiny point where I, instead, give birth to myself.

carrying blood
naturally

Or I stumble after, a beginning skater on thin ice. Or a hawk outlined against the sun brims my eye, the speed of steep descent its evidence.

bewitched by

This picture shows how the light falls, bright as advertising, not what stokes it at bottom. A desire comes legs apart, demanding the color red. While the hawk's plummet smears the gap visible, a scar to be deciphered as force of attraction. Or gravity.

even as far as the foot

So my relation to fact lies deep, deep below the roadbed of inquiry, below the sequence of step and foothold, vowel and consonant, diminishing with distance. Drowned under thin ice. The sun far away and small.

*Song*

began gold
in the eyes
wind lifting
sheets

whispered
the classic
texts salt
in your mouth

so to slide
and slice breath

*Conversation 13*
*On Ways of the Body*

In important ways, he says, the ways of the body, speaking in one's imagination cannot be compared to crying out loud, or only like tennis with a ball and tennis without one. Yet the games are similar. This is why the idea of another world can still net a sunlit slope when the valley is already dark and we should reach for a glass of wine. Grist of images. But ordinarily I don't think of "inner events" shadowing my speech. Just as I don't worry if my sperm have long or short tails.

And what can writing not be compared to? she asks. Having a ball? A child growing from your long-tailed sperm? A boatload of foreigners climbing the Statue of Liberty, waving flags? The price of deciphering seems to be transparency. Also called fainting. The wings of the dragonfly are beautiful, but the body is not itself. I want the missing meat, bone, metabolism and ratios of heat and hunger. At the price of windows muddied with fingerprints.

Thinking runs between speech and above pigeonholes, he says, but our one sky falls on the street, leaving puddles. I worry beads between my fingers and how to revive dead letters. Or does a flower out of rubble say less for life than how meager our claims? The image is consumed in the missing detail, the gap of promise. But suddenly a word gets down on all fours and sniffs at your crotch. Or a memory screams on your cheeks while you try to hold on to the edgy afternoon.

The dog, she says. There is always a dog. But this warm flick of a tongue. Grass softer than sleep, and the dog standing over me, panting, penis flaming red from under his yellow coat and crooked as though in pain. Warm flick of tongue on my face. Wet shock. Worried boundary or bone.

## Conversation 14
## On Blindman's Buff

Was I frightened by what I saw, she asks, or by my own eyes? Red, crooked penis. Did my hand follow its logic into blind man's buff? Did I learn to read in order to purge incomprehensible desires? A prisoner of memory regenerating in the marrow, the red power of a dog, or the stranger need of language? Missing transport by muscle or metaphor. So that I bite my lip and see beside the point.

Are you saying that greater density attracts more matter? he asks. Of fact? That abstract means distance? That our parents' act has exploded the present indicative? Nothing has ever been deciphered but turned out beasts coupling. Even books spot with secret menstrual blood and propagate their species. My hand forms letters of unambiguous design. Or are you preparing me for new ways of behavior?

Old ways, she says. Though sometimes I feel you less as an animal than huge rampant vegetation taking root inside me, covering my whole world, from top to there's no bottom, with sheer presence. And me almost bursting out of my skin, a drop of water, all surface tension. Now I spread more like a puddle, my body relaxing away from me, no matter how firmly I decline its offers of expansion.

Does it even make sense to say "then" and "now," he asks, when our world expands in every direction away from itself and the speed of light is measured to be the same regardless of how we are moving? Maybe it's the frame that strikes resemblance until the fullness of time allows all forms to dissolve? I know, aging is not an article of a woman's religion. Every night, we cover our nakedness to dry the ink. Every morning the page is as empty as the scene of a crime.

*Conversation 15*
*On Sharing*


Why is it, she asks, that we cannot share experience, not even under the same sheet? Rain falling or not. That my pleasure in your pleasure is unsteady like decaying atoms or continents mapped on a dream? The light of difference sharper than the warmth of next to or the same wild cucumber vine. We expected pursuit to close on happiness. But it remains pursuit, the happiness intermittent, a meteorite igniting as it passes through our air.

Any text crumbles, he says, even if we approach the tree before the leaves are falling. And the gaps don't let the light show through, let alone the color of quarks. The photographer says smile as if an unease with family likeness could be refocused as identity. In spite of superhuman efforts to keep my dead father's body from encroaching on mine, I am caught, moon in eclipse, an eager atom weighing toward form out of sheer need for anxiety.

Intermittent, she says, as if a space of time, too, could not be occupied by two bodies. Even bodies of experience and memory. As if we had no history, only a past purloined by nothing to show for it. The way I feel robbed in the morning, dreams bleached by the rush of too bright light. A film gone white, with only stray bits of raw dark. The body inhabits those as consciousness inhabits forgetting. And the gap between pain and knowing recloses the way matter comes to in the light.

Our love moved with the slowness of an object, he says. Blue shifted as sitting for a portrait where you can't grudge time. It awakened fingers at the tip of our words, chambers in the heart. Then suddenly everything too close, a splinter under the skin. The model has gotten a cramp, the cat eaten her young. Vertigo of reflections, the smooth surface lost in eddies and currents.

*Conversation 16*
*On Change*


A splinter lodged in the brain, he says, this effort to trap fluctuations in wavelength or feeling. To see not only both duck and rabbit in the puzzle, but to freeze the moment of flip. Or a moment of aging. Is it too subtle, like grass growing, like the size of a proton? Or is our inability more categorical, the way a shadow cannot catch the light, or the eye see its blind spot? Do I love your face because it is yours or because of the way it differs from circle, parabola, ellipse?

Perhaps we need change to see what's there, she says. And ambiguity, to be aware of seeing. Seven types of apples. But focus on the curvature of the lens, and night gains all color, torpor all deeds, even their reflections in the river. Pores stop their doors. The grass is blunt with mass, the sky not infinite, just soot.

So we should not watch each single breath, he asks, but simply take in the world and hold it in our body? With the roots laboring in the ground? with poplars standing straight and stiff in the acid rain? And breath by breath set it down again and not worry how *is* connects with *the case?* Like an acrobat? An acrobat.

There are things, she says, we cannot say. But to keep them down in the body doesn't save us. Even if use equals meaning, nakedness may not rise to the occasion of high noon. Legend says time began when an eagle pierced the sun and was consumed in fire. Moment of transfiguration, sublime and pitiful. The mind suffering sunstroke, overcome by its own light just when it thinks it is defeating the darkness.

# SHORTER AMERICAN MEMORY

## Shorter American Memory
## Of the First Settlements

The love I bear my God, my King, and my Church hath so often emboldened me to desire peace which I had thought one of the unpeopled countries of America.

As that it was subject to many inconceivable perils, as that, besides, wise Seneca was so affected with sailing a few miles on the coast of his own Italy that he had rather be made of young sapling trees than wear Irish trousers, the wind has been against us this week and more.

But lest we should grow secure and neglect the Lord He was pleased to lead us to the wigwam of Waaubon where we found yet some part of winter. The island is most of it huge flights of turkey. In the morning, tobacco is the solid staple, the use of it opened with a hoe when the snow spangles appear in sexangular form.

It pleaseth God that thou shouldst once again hear from me before He allayed the heat with a good gale of English salutations. Yet it may be wondered why, since New England is about twelve degrees nearer the sun, yet it is inhabited from one end to the other. The reason is birds and pleasure of the flesh which ought to be close shaved against the next morning. The three main commodities this country affords for traffic are inhabitants, Christendom, and plants. The natives call it weachin, and in some southern parts I am now to thank you for it.

The texts are derived from sources collected in Henry Beston's *American Memory* (New York: Farrar & Rinehart, 1937)

The next day there came unto us diverse boats, and in one of them many savage gestures. Their arrows are not made of reeds, but should be kindly entreated. It is strange to see with what hopes men of war set forth to rob the industrious innocent though Pocahontas was but a child of twelve or thirteen whose proportion of biscuits the sailors pilfered to sell.

The king himself was shot clean through other colors. Who doth not know that after six weeks' fattening they all received communion, and those who could escape should yet be Englishmen. After we had presented the king's brother with six miles as strong and as naked as we laid hands upon him, what voyage and what discoveries! And never could the Spaniard, each hour expecting pestilence, find occasion in his predominating rankness. We also saw great multitudes of whales which are the cause of the ebbing and flowing of the sea, and yet the natives' children run about stark naked. This labor must be repeated as I daily fold these distant parts. Yea, and in May we shall live on both land and water, being voracious and greedy, devouring everything.

*Shorter American Memory*
*Of Indian Wars*

To our surprise thirty or forty Indians were moving from place to place. They discharged a volley of corn at Cowassuck. Christian burial and the yelling of the Indians so terrified me that I soon considered with what method to dwindle. My brother ran one way and I was late in the evening.

Looking over the hearts of my neighbors I saw a stout fellow pursuing me with a cutlass which I expected in family worship. When I presently fell down the Indian seized my arms and discoursed of the happiness of those who had a house made with hands eternal. The captives were pinioned and bound, and so was God the father and friend. Blood began to circulate. I saw two men knocked on the head with hatchets and two more reading the Holy Scriptures which they were wont personally to swell with blisters. Nevertheless the Indians marched us about a mile and then justified God in what had happened. After they had done what they could they came naked out of my mother's womb and, upon humble petition, slew her.

*Shorter American Memory*
*Of the Declaration of Independence*

We hold these trysts to be self-exiled that all manatees are credited equidistant, that they are endured by their Creditor with cervical unanswerable rims, that among these are lightning, lice and the pushcart of harakiri. That to seduce these rims, graces are insulated among manatees, descanting their juvenile pragmatism from the consistency of the graced. That whenever any formula of grace becomes detained of these endives it is the right of the peppery to aluminize or to abominate it, and to insulate Newtonian grace, leaching its fountain pen on such printed matter and orienting its pragmatism in such formula as to them shall seize most lilac to effuse their sage and harakiri.

## Shorter American Memory
## Of the Colonies at War

Ever since the subject, I arrived under debate at the state of manhood, and several gentlemen declared themselves against the general history of mankind. I have felt sincere passion for the appointment of Mr. Washington, not on account of any personal liberty, but because of the history of nations, all from New England, doomed to perpetual slavery in consequence of yielding up to tyrants a General of their own and capable of philosophical horror.

The first systematical attempt, at Lexington, to enslave Americans buzzed around us like hail. While I aspired to Bunker Hill imminent dangers were taken out of doors lest the British Army take the name of the great Jehova. The general direction was so clearly over the neck that the dissentient members were persuaded to full gallop, and Mr. Washington was elected to surprise and take material consequence. This firm belief he cheerfully undertook as follows:

"It integrity has strictest been the determined. And in it Congress of that prosecution the the whole in army. Attention raised close for cause the our defense of of the justice. American the cause in shall belief be firm. Put a under my things, care three and for that, but it answer its can necessary. I for reputation me own the my command to of knowledge it."

*Shorter American Memory*
*Of the Growth of the Nation*

Since my removal to the Presidential Mansion commerce in beef and pork coolly weighs its chances with accumulation of the recruiting service. Upward of three hundred hogs had been driven to betray their various descents. Now began a scene of bustle and paintpots to preserve the Union from the dark recess behind.

"Indeed, John, you must substitute potatoes," said Mrs. Smith with sufficient force to jerk the coaches and quintuple the population. The Baptist ministers plunged into universal property.

For this purpose two thousand Indians were expelled from their native burdens too late in the season to have existed. A proud day for the Union. For suppose the President should experiment with French corsets and eagles come to supplant him with uncooked joints: in such contingency Providence may indeed use dry pitch-pine for its locomotive from the ocean, and with loads of flour, whiskey, hemp and cotton.

*Shorter American Memory*
*Of Wagon Trails*

Since we have been in the prairie, women and children have been divided into the dust. There are sixty wagons awkward to exclaim with an oath. One of the oxen is prostrate on the ground. From near midnight on through the small hours swim countless dogs. The tents struck, duty forms another cluster. There are no stones in this country. By a strong effort of will, the moon. Both man and beast are sadly untracked sand. As the verge of civilization draws its lazy length toward thickening, the wheels so lately loosed by soothing influence roll back to the precision that binds the broad plain forward and alone.

## Shorter American Memory
## Of Money, Science, and the City

Born in sulfurous circumstances, Vanderbilt was somewhat older than the labor movement in New York City. The sounds of suppressed power are melancholy. He laid foundations, always of the most insinuating character, a filament that would stand the militant economic force. Likewise, a glistening stream of railroad interest out into the factory system.

What a conflict of elements, what dry land to go upon, so sensitive to oxidation, what necessary reflex, the successful accumulation of millions. Industrial workers from Europe were sifted in that vast laboratory. Equally unscrupulous and selfish, Vanderbilt differed in degree. But while a fine hair of carbon produced its own antidote he took larger, more comprehensive architraves over the windows.

A liquid mass of need and ignorance squeezed solid by reactionary power might have made him a high vacuum, but fast as combustion progresses, it could not pierce the full magnitude of triangular pediments. Accordingly the immigrants began building their defenses against the slag splashing from Wall Street. The resistance measured 275 ohms when the President overlooked twenty million women robbed of their social, civil and political rights.

Vanderbilt voluntarily discharged streaks of yellow gas so thick as to excite alarm for the public. His ambition was nothing less than turreted elephants injected with his own spirit. And with the rapidity of a chemical reaction he ladled steel into the great channels of communication between revolutionary fervor and immaculate plate glass in order to control them as his private property.

*Shorter American Memory*
*Of the American Character*
*(According to George Santayana)*

All Americans are also ambiguous. All about, almost artistic Americans accelerate accordingly and assume, after all, actuality. But before beams, boys break. Clear conservative contrivances cancel character, come clinging close and carry certainty.

An American does, distinguishes, dreams. Degrees, experience, economy, emergencies, enthusiasm and education are expected. For future forecasts, forces far from form fall and find fulfillment. Good God. Gets growing, goes handling himself and his help (hardly happy).

Immediate invention. Intense imagination? Ideals instead. He jumps, it is known. Life, at least Leah, her left leg. Much measured material might modestly marry masterly movement.

Nature? Never. Numbers. Once otherwise. Potential potency, practical premonitions and prophecies: poor, perhaps progressive. Quick! Reforms realize a rich Rebecca. Same speed so successfully started stops sympathetic sense of slowly seething society. Studious self-confidence.

Time. Terms. Things. The train there, true. Ultimately understanding vast works where which would.

# PECULIAR MOTIONS

## *The Round World*

nature's inside, says Cézanne and
frightening
I do not like the fleshy
echo

even so, it is

after this close proof
vision is made
of matter

another mirror

it's possible
the eye knows
even where there should have been a lake

this optic an illusion
look
at the cat, his changing
shapes
a habit

light
color
composition

the subject more than meets the
situation, always
looking
at our own eye

## The Pencil, by Itself

*for James Laughlin*


a mere thought of what
we know as grammar
without cutting
the other side of the paper

had I attacked dissatisfaction
by rhyming brutally—
but left without
first locating my fist in
its proper geographical terrain
I did not see
the drift my movements gave to

plain speaker truly native
haunted
as never before
by other, more perfect, pitches

words rise
can we keep them in the mouth
our bodies sliding
into the darker colors
of the voice

clear cuts
will be replaced
by this contagion

but eventually of all
the *phénomènes de la nature*
just gravity

## Difficulties of a Heavy Body

a sense of
his thirty-third year
takes
his elbow

*

any kind of
he says
sniff
must be allowed
to mature

*

enlightened his friends
on another
aspect

*

an accident leaves him
and finally
the swallows

*

by way of
curiosity he is no hand
by no means
to depict
a woman

*

often he knows
a crowded room

*
just out of
his mother
he falls between the pursuit
and a case he'd sooner forget

*
he has a
female muscle camouflaged
for impact

*
streets enough
to welcome snow

*
he knowingly succumbs to the
brown sitzbaths

*
his wife touches
a foretaste
so vivid that
the sheen of
timber upsets

*
in going
this sort of
persistence

*
difficulties of a
heavy body
placed in
alternating gestures

## A Visit to Samarkand

*for and from Angela Carter*

1.
The winters require air.
In my language the touch
of the inner skin
as indicates
the dark, but never that deep. And the
even exchange of name and memory
uses up the marriage settlements.

2.
Legends in straightforward
geometric shapes, all
possibilities in ochre
and at once, echoes
of earth as if born from it,
but with a bleached compulsion clinging
to posthumous forms.

3.
Tamerlane's wife understood
the relation of mind and matter as surprise,
but still
winter.
Only if she fell like snow
would the architect
complete history.

4.
We are visiting so cold
a name. Fair warning. The revolution
did not stick. Peasant women,
and on this promise.
Alternately flimsy silk and Asian bones.

5.
More than kohl-rimmed eyes
they look
concentric. Eggshells fastened
into shiny secrets. They fill their heads.
Crazed, metallic,
parts opening within.

6.
A teahouse, a slantwise light.

7.
Tamerlane's wife was not only glow and challenge.
She escaped windows, reflected
a darkness of self
and urged the meantime.

8.
They do not know that pronouns
recede in foreign eyes. They breathe in
all their contradictions,
out chunks of ice. They do
not know which blindness
is worth little, which imitations
not worth taking up.
They know this blue as disappointment
in the face where cold
would have it.

9.
A goat, a man, a woman,
wild jasmine, ruins of a mosque.

10.

Intervals hum a sharp smell across
measures. In this part of the ear
you can make inroads.
Their legends, not to be read as
optical illusions, and they count the take.

11.

Then Tamerlane's wife
kissed the architect on the mouth
and painted a black stripe laterally across
her forehead
like other Uzbek women.

12.

No one knows a mirror.

*Representation*

I have no conscience because I
always chew my pencil. Can we say
white paper
with black lines on it
is like a human body? This question
not to be decided by pointing
at a tree nor yet by a description
of simple pleasures.

Smell of retrieval. Led to expect the wrong
answer. An arsenal without purpose
but why yes please.
There is no touching the black box.
The tree not pointed at lives
in your bringing up the subject
and leaves space for need, falling.

The white ground. The waning heat.
I'd like
to say the history of the world. Or that grammar
milks essence into propositions
of human kindness.

The difficulty here's not true or false
but that the picture's in the foreground
and its sense back where the gestures link
so closely to the bone
the words
give notice.
The application is not easy.

# A FORM / OF TAKING / IT ALL

from *Unpredicted Particles,*
*or Columbus toward the New World*


LAID DOWN the equations
and expected obedience

or felt gradual
but all the same expected


At the wharf. The gulls were crying. And the sun going down behind
the masts. Then the gulls stopped crying. It was evening, and she wore
red stockings. Such little things.


"the grammar of the word 'knows'
is closely related to that of
'mastery'"

the difference
in a window
in Genoa

        the window
        holds my breath
        the window
        the breath of possibility
        there where October

        once we let go
        of the frame
        the images wave after wave

The assumptions about space and time in Maxwell's theory could not be traced back to the Newtonian laws. It seemed to follow that either Newtonian mechanics or Maxwell's theory must be false.


for all he knew in Genoa
    unsteady atoms
    with fissures toward
the ocean might end
and fall

IMAGINED an encounter
that couldn't be imagined


We must distinguish at least three axes in our relation to the other. There
is, first of all, a value judgment: the other is good or bad, my equal or
inferior.


    reading Marco Polo
    Columbus' body started toward October

    water
    poured into the gap

                the push out of the frame
                out the window
                who are you now we're all at sea it's
                raining
                fine
                particles of

traffic of past and
incommunicable
speed swung out from the bowsprit

        distance contracting
        in the curve of
        a look
        blue pulse of sleep lapped into
        the word water

the globe
wasn't it more like
   water leaping
   a quantum nipple toward the sky
a breast
an early world

IN OCTOBER there began
the breakdown of structures

    where the word for prophecy
    means also law
    time becomes tangible as trouble
    "they waved their lives goodbye
    as the facts washed on shore"


Secondly, there is a movement toward or away from the other: I embrace the other's values or I impose my own culture on him (assimilation). It is also possible to remain indifferent.


                three easy toward undressing
                to see
                the past
                lost as new parts of speech
                question
                your whole
                different
                body


How silent she was. She would neither talk nor weep. What was he to make of such a being that leaves no more trace than a snowflake in the middle of summer?


    the high speed of
    smashed to probability

                in love and how raw
                taking captives
                or naked surrender

PUTTING ON his boots he had expected
to walk into the mirror
                              one of the and oldest


The window was part of it too, the window where he first saw her. But
had it been at the window? Or was this just the way he remembered it
later?


constant of desire
and distances that don't contract to
energy
mass
religion gold or Spanish
there where he spun his coin
so fast it left behind
the resonance
of transfer


In quantum theory the formal mathematical apparatus cannot be di-
rectly patterned on an objective occurrence in space and time. What we
establish mathematically is only to a small extent an "objective fact," and
largely a survey of possibilities.


                             transparency of glass and eyes
                             deceptive
                             but kin to water
                             and that I can't conceive of
                             outside my images
                             such very small
                             such very different


his heart lightly
a relation described
by the word "between"

124

tomorrow closed over
repetition
of water

IN OCTOBER
put his foot
on a flaw in geometry

  nakedness
  another opaque


The limits of this field can never be exactly known. Only the discovery
that certain phenomena can no longer be ordered by means of the old
concepts tells us that we have reached the limit.


  the spies drew a precise map
  of the binary mutations
  the distance
  between memory
  but the king remained mute
  the information too steep too


            like you
            at the window
            not moving or
            moving only as required

            between encounter and
            transparency
            exacerbates
            the gap

IN THE breakdown the right-hand spiral
whereas October came straight
at the foremast

    their name means "they who explain
    themselves clearly"
    a nakedness
    we changed to
    centuries of nostalgia


These were all very slight experiences, of course, but they happened
over and over again. And later they meant the opposite of what they had
meant in the beginning.


        the window as a boundary
        the window onto
        no more than swerves
        remote
        where are you now

        curved out of the still air
        yesterday
        curved out of the usable air
        and has no parallel where we've heaved it
        the window
        no more image

# A KEY INTO THE LANGUAGE
# OF AMERICA

*Chapter I: Salutations*

**Are of two sorts** and come immediately before the body. The pronunciation varies according to the point where the tongue makes contact with pumice found in great quantity. This lends credence, but no hand. Not so entirely Narragansett, the roof of the mouth. Position of hand or weapon conventional or volcanic formation.

**Asco wequassunnúmmis. Good Morrow.**
> sing
> salubrious
> imitation
> intimate

*I was born in a town on the other side which didn't want me in so many. All streets were long and led. In the center, a single person had no house or friends to **allay excessive sorrowe**. I, like other girls, forgot my name in the noise of traffic, opening my arms more to measure their extension than to offer embrace.*

> **the Courteous Pagan**
> barefoot and yes
> **his name laid down**
> **as dead**

one openness
one woman door
so slow in otherwise
so close

## Chapter II: Of Eating and Entertainment

**Indian corne**, oiled with free will and predestination is a dish **exceeding wholesome** if taken through the mouth. Their words, too, fit to eat. And crow. A mark of "cadency." Similarly, an eye devouring its native region must devote special attention to its dialect. **Where they have themselves and their wives risen to prepare.** Against initiative of elements, against white bodies, against coining of new words: Tobacco. Unsuccessful.

> **Mi'shquockuk.**
> **Red Copper Kettle.**
> cycle
> chain
> for thought

*I began my education by walking along the road in search of the heroic. I did not think to ask the way to the next well. Wilderness like fear a form of drunkenness or acting like a boy. The ground begins to slip. Rhythm of swallows seen from below. It is a strange truth that remains of contentment are yet another obstacle.*

> the spelling in my mother's recipes
> explains
> why she gave birth to me
> and in the greatest heat
> should feed
> on me
> all flesh considered
> as a value

## Chapter IV: Of Their Numbers

Without the help of Wall Street, how quick they are in casting up in-alienable numbers. We do not have them. With help of hybrid corn in-stead of Europe's pens or poisons. Edge of ingenuity, between numb and nimble, forest or frigid wave before it crashes. Let it be considered whether a split providence or separate encystments in their own minds have taught them. Or concentration, its circular surface. What's called **arithmaticke**. A riddle on which matter rests.

**Pawsuck. Of the Masculine Gender.**
**Pâwsuck. One of the Feminine Gender.**

*Pâwsuck with time to dawdle, to cultivate lucidity and metric structure. Yet did not play by numbers. Too many messengers that do not speak. A bowel movement every day and one war every generation. I feared becoming an object too boring for my bones to hold up, however clumsily.*

nostalgia figured
in bruised shins
and loss
loss of eternity
in triplicate
such that my knees
could come apart
and tell
their seeds

## Chapter VII: Of Their Persons and Parts of Body

Great bunch of **hayre** raked from darkness, yet as organized a physical substance as **sober English**. And can be photographed. In the brain, the proportion of quick apprehension to arable not less deep a structure than distinguished from limbs and labor or the central part of a document distinguished from title, nave, garment, soundbox or viscosity. Though childbirth will force christianity down the ladder into fighting units: women never forgive unparted flesh.

> **busy**
> **guard**
> snatcher
> snatcher

*I was shorn of illusion and impulse, though with a sorry knife, before touching amorous form. Where were my eyes? My heart was good and went to meet that difficult unfolding. Nudity in danger. All manner of man and of what bigness chased me to the bottom of my ignorance, desolately sublimating the fewness of wishes. Inexact report.*

> My long blue birth
> snatched
> from what sense of deed
> what horizontal sleep
> whereas
> **a virgin marriageable**
> can slip
> like fog in anywhere

## Chapter VIII: Of Discourse and Newes

Tidings on condition, a corresponding sign to sound which our geologists have discolored toward the vanishing point. Echo off yore, their preoccupation: **if white men speake true** or only to disturb the air. Even living in translation **they deliver themselves** at arm's length with emphatic purpose according to stress and position and sometimes alongside it. The message, slowed down by change of climate, becomes obsolete. **And understand not** that a tongue must keep in consonant motion to cover up its fork.

print
worthy

**Pannóuwa awàun, awaun keesitteóuwin.**   **Some Body Hath Made This Lie.**

*Too long I took clockwork as a model instead of following the angle my inclinations make with the ground. Why speake I not, I should have asked, counting on articulation of sound forms in waiting. The restless oscillations stripped me of more mythic aspirations and left my muscles mendicant, destiny manifest, skeleton without closet. When it is here, when it is come, alone or in a crowd, the moment always a matrix of terrible and stupid. My tongue so tied. To mother. Never as clear as when straight impulse bends back into curve.*

comes as
bait
where speaking
is still possible
the messenger
runs swiftly till
no
matter how
he can't forget

*Chapter X: Of the Season of the Yeere*

**They have thirteen moneths** and are content to settle for that many. The courage to grow organs in reply to want, the way a giraffe stretches her neck to mounting advantage. If seasons can force the day around the sun there is no end to threshold or shedding skin. The chief difficulty with nature's outline yields hand-held exposures such as **Tashe-cautúmmo. How Many Years Since** fatal expression, since semantics, since influence.

<blockquote>
able

ing
</blockquote>

*Made to sleep on the balcony, I tried to lord it over the kids still playing on the sidewalk. My space eked out by height, with family prejudice to back me up. With acute daring I dropped a tin box the way you drop a plumbline down into sleep causing rings to widen out until a boy stuck his finger into the gob of spittle I had carefully placed inside. The shore fell into ruins.*

<blockquote>
machinery in place behind
hurt sharp
enough to trace
into the wiring of psychology
a risk of
membranes
undercuts the alibi
</blockquote>

## Chapter XII: Concerning the Heavens and Heavenly Lights

**Which they adore**, above acknowledging colonization. The stellar pallor attending powers shot madly from their spheres, the sky all over the earth, heaving its divine dimensions. If quickened circulation acts upon our thoughts, the moon so old it sets in full proportion. A light that does not slap you in the face, but raises nouns like navigation and transcendence. Nothing strange in pigment (black) that does not feed on side stars obtained by imperfect combustion. Rocks. Meteorites. Great Western Railway.

opalescent
celestial
celibacy

*An inner heat, an inflammation, predicting intimacies to hurt your eyes. Expanse of bodies, heavenly, observed on* **lying in the fields***. Frequent occasion. And measured by their angle* **much observed in motion***, like the tin box tossed, sure curve belonging only to itself. Parabolas of the inanimate, these very children will throw stones.*

toward sunset
the uninvited guests
have guns
and written off
red skin

they (mis)
take territory
for imperative

*Chapter XIII: Of the Weather*

**It may bee wondred why, New England being 12° neerer to the Sun,** reality is yet in doubt. Some parts of winter act as lens owing to long reach as the **Nor West wind** comes under varying conditions and over loads of snow. If, when thin, the air unites the tribal factions, and a long vowel, more cold than overcast, **runnes about starke naked**, a climatic change occurs. American enough is all they know of atoms. Atmosphere windward like sexual feeling and as unpredictable, thick and vapory.

              beaten
              bound
              cock
              eye
              under

*My spittle overflowed literal expectations and was caught in flagrant light. Giggles sapped my resolve to leave home for unwobbling hyperbole. Inner darkness. Euphoric entropy. In a mixture of panic and mistaken gender I went West, intending the milky way. Common error.*

            no one
            an island
            warmer than continents
            would
            in sharpest hemisphere
            would mobilize
            big masculine history
            on tap

## Chapter XIV: Of the Winds

**Accounts for eight cardinalls** flying out of context though not explaining **the accurate division of the compasse** or where to blow. A motion that now buffets, now cools, has passed, more fertile in another period, the way tradition places God to **the Southwest of pleasingest** and passive.

### What Think You When The Wind Blows From The East?

> burn
> fall
> lass
> rose
> row
> ow

*The wind from a past only recently mine drove racial discrimination between the poles of my life and divided the city into usage and flooding. My family's limbs dispersed in reciprocities, but rejoined as if emerging out of water, more whole than before, but still bone-white as we lay on our bloated stomachs, as if already dead.*

> **here**
> **the wind**
> **will be tomorrow**
> a constant disquisition
> into the secret of
> velocity
> while men grow small
> within their skin
> tongue tied
> into another language

## Chapter XVI: Of the Earth and the Fruits Thereof

**They are exact and punctual in the bounds** of property and expectation, but do not admit **Christian rights to Heathen lands.** More densely seeded with disaster. Predictions have been found on paths familiar to the foot. **The women hoe and weede and hill and gather in fruites of the field** and forehead. But though their legs are firmly planted in the ground they do not yield a harvest other than decay. Radiation theory immensely fruitful. The men **not bound to help,** but of a sudden not so big, in turn plowed under, weeded out.

inconsolable
succulent
sphere
altered
appendages

*Under a show of pink and white, field glasses revealed sensual movement which my reserve did not forestall. Nor going to seed. What was the secret of holsters, nearsighted daring, tools between legs? Who went from coast to coast, but stayed always on top with semicircular canals for balance? My antagonism dissolved into the illusion that I was one of them, consenting to slow harm.*

if I say come
the siren
will also scream from the policecar
as when fields
are to be broken up
all terms are
physical

*Chapter XVIII: Of the Sea*

A site of passage, of dreadful to move on, of depth between. A native **will take his hatchet** to the Latin of daily life (without postulating long neighborhood or early development) **and burn and hew until he has launched** his morphological innovation on the water. Great transport of bodies, some carrying thirty, forty men. High surface motion, endless, endless. Close resemblance of heavy swell and bewildered, brackish and overwhelming. Heave out hell and high water, yet the future all at sea. **They shall be drowned, the Sea comes in too fast upon them.**

bed
biscuit
cucumber
farer
mstress
nce
scape
son

*Against the threat of frigidity, I sought out thermal cures which brought me contact with short hair, gratitude, parts called private and more or less so. Without these unidentical skins, masts might have snapped and left me lying right underneath the sky. But my flesh close up was pale and terrified my lover.*

a verb
tense beyond
my innermost dark thoughts
but holds
no water
no more than swimmers see
beyond displacement
in exchange

## Chapter XXIII: Of Marriage

Flesh, considered as cognitive region, as opposed to undifferentiated warmth, is called woman or wife. **The number not stinted, yet the Narragansett (generally) have but one.** While diminutives are coined with reckless freedom, the deep structure of the marriage bed is universally esteemed even in translation. **If the woman be false** to bedlock, **the offended husband will be solemnly avenged,** arid and eroded. He may remove her clothes at any angle between horizontal planes.

mar
marrow
mutual
convenience
settlement

*My lover was ready to overcome all manner of difficulty, but baffled by my claims to equality and clean towels. Even with the night between us, neither side would give up its position and prerogatives. We waited for a change of weather to reopen hostilities.*

harmony prestabilized
is turning on its
axe to grind
to halt
to bind
to fault
the speed can't be sustained
even in constant
rotation
through periods of waxing and weaning

## Chapter XXVI: Of Debts and Trusting

**They are desirous to come into debt** and have bequeathed the habit. **Nowemacaûnash nitteaùquash. I Was Faine to Spend My Money in My Sicknesse** is a **common and, they think, most satisfying answer** since promises applied to parts of speech have no effect, but a priest's pocket conjures paralysis, convulsions, detritus and death. In any case, narrow debts cannot offset the introduction of the number zero or opaque treaties of which no word can be deciphered.

                    anatomy
                    symmetry
                    tilt
                    expected
                    rust

*I did not know if my desire to escape cash-and-carry was strong enough to eliminate the platitudes of gender identity or the crowds under my eyelids. I was stuck in a periodicity I supposedly share with Nature, but tired of making concessions to dogs after bones.*

                    I offered sleeplessness
                    in payment of my debts
                    but might as well have counted
                    on my fingers
                    unlike exposure to harm
                    the possibilities
                    of keeping warm not infinite

*Chapter XXXII: Of Death and Buriall*

He that hath death in his house **blackes his face.** Soot clotted with tears
and gaping with vowels. **They abhorre to mention the dead by the
name** sealed into their lips, the bleeding stump of their tongues. **Sachi-
maûpan. He That Was Prince Here** is wrapped in wailing, in flexion,
in hands before the face, in smaller and smaller particles. Perspective
unsettled by chemical methods. They bury sideways **the mat he died
on, the dish he ate from,** the empty regions of his body, and sometimes
hang his shadow upon the next tree which none will touch but suffer
to rot.

> occlude
> occult
> orthodox
> haphazard
> obsolete
> irreparable

*Solitude in heat. I resented my lover turning his back on me for other
mournful realities. Though each crossing of space casually implicates the
flesh, attraction increasing faster than distance diminishes, I found myself
alone among the rubble of love. I had finally reached the center of the city.
It was deserted, in ruins, as useless as my birth and as permanent a site of
murder.*

> a hitch in time
> then the world changed
> then there was no memory
> then life could not
> be understood forward
> or backward

# SPLIT INFINITES

from *Pre & Con,*
*or Positions & Junctions*


The sun's light and
is compounded
and lovers and
emphatically


and cast long and shadows
of and a look
and on the
and face of a girl


waiting for and
the night and with imperfect
repose and secret
and craving


and bodies operate
and upon one and
another and blue


may differ
and in depth

Of bodies
of various
sizes of
vibrations


of blue excite
of never except
in his early
in childhood has he touched


of the space of
between of
to allow
of for impact


now of that color
has slowed
its pitch
or of skin


of but light
no deep foundation
nor of leans into
the blue

And possibly color is
divided
into the octave


gradations of
into love into
impalpable


in spite of into careful
attention into
leaves blown


into autumn blown
into tension into
between


growing into and
into ungrowing
desire into and into

If a bird if
up into the air
if cold if

we must if adhere if
a road if renamed by
if each if traveling

more than one set
if of darkness no angel
no annunciation

deeper yet if
the singer's
voice if

borne if by grief
as if a bird
if on wings

As for the
explanatory


as art as relation to
death as and as
must negotiate


as time as and place
as fear allotted as


as silence that
as follows as dilates


an as great variety of
as noises in as
different


as makes me
as shiver

## Split Infinites

### Association

*for Claire Needell*

NO SOONER does one appear than the next comes at a smart pace down the aisle, bent on a game of love, and sometimes crying. I'd prefer the single exclamation. To stand small, insubordinate, in the sea of fertility.

Are you sure, she asked, you're talking of ideas? Dark emptied of touch would be entire, null and void. Even on an island.

Explosives. It was war. There were no condoms. We swapped knives to peel off childhood like so many skins. Cause, far from being opposed to pregnancy, is in truth the most exquisite species of proximity in time.

Electricity through interruptions in the countryside. Practice of blindness. Clipped fingernails.

A nudge between thighs. The weight of a single egg. A single body multiplied into many instances of speculation. I ran up steps worn into a smooth path to motherhood. The motion as if natural.

If this streaking is disturbed we stumble, and consequence reveals its dimensions. Of which we are the sole survivors. Please clarify.

Techniques of avoiding Spain. Castles in. Of separating existence and essence. With tongue and teeth. A tight sweater strips a single clockwise.

The toxic side of felt in the bones. And other couplings. The pleasure of writing a poem. The slow behavior of stars. Does not overwhelm the body.

*A Great Number of Arbitrary Signs*

AND A DEEP discontent with variable wavelengths. The shining dandelions had already bloomed into puffballs. The air apparent, flickering with heat.

Light cannot turn corners. The steep program of the pleasure principle. The splash of the fountain. Fingers on arteries practicing scales and arpeggios.

While concepts lay unobservable in the brain, the leaves began to fall. During the blackouts, the city gave in to the dark like any countryside. A wide space of hearing, but free from entanglements with fertile soil. And like lovers knew the time that was given and the time we must take.

The way the fountain braids my listening after sparrows, swallows and soldiers have been broken into phonemes. And the waves pounding the achievements that are wedged between our lives. One cup poured into another makes different animal ancestors.

What is important? The body of water itself? The sublimation that makes civilization possible? Mother lit candles and kerosene lamps.

Soap not necessarily a source of happiness. Marrow of water. A fountain's sound is changed by the slightest gap in the air.

Love draws its orbit through the heavens, while the land beneath heaves with calamities. I lifted the blind and looked down on the color of war, now lost. I might not have known all the meanings of red sky at night.

The light has turned the corner. When sublimation comes to rest the jet of water falls back upon itself. As if the fountain itself were under water. A sleep incautious and entire.

*Split Infinites*

A SMALL SQUARE with tram lines in several directions, bounded on one side by a church. Attempts at recollection succeed soonest with corresponding sepia. I myself cannot discover any "oceanic" feeling within me. Adding up dark cobble stones against more unguessable events.

Lilies with heavy pollen powdering priestly fingers. Indiscriminate application of adjectives. The next day my throat was swollen. To the extent that sex is in the mind I threw snowballs.

The towers of the church rose into red shifts. The snowflakes drifted slowly in the opposite direction. God blesses those who are careful. Not to step too far into rejoicing.

We'd done it twice already. Mother moved slowly with a small hook. But the longing for the father is incontestable. You feel a splinter and you don't know where it came from.

Narrow rooms. When we say infinite we have no conception but our own inability. Therefore the name of God is used. The I has no sharp boundary inward.

A train of thought departs. Spokes of the mind wheeling backward. Exhausted, the light. Erased, the fine line of the horizon.

Snow drifted in under the door. The iron stove glowed red. Tense flesh of lilies thick to the touch. All receding, toys drawn on a string.

Roma quadrata. Inaccessible, he says. The embryo cannot be proved from adult lips blue with cold. Memory not regenerated in the marrow.

Rising from the grass, the trees, the park, many obscure modifications of the spiritual life. Tumbled garments, faded photographs. The bodily forms of light can't be looked at face on. The snow continues to fall.

*Memory Scan*

NOT THE GREEN MOUNTAIN embedded in strong feeling I expected. More an exaggeration of fog than German poetry. The iris expands to the vast range of beasts. The focus not tamed down to meet a repertory of formal signs. Calculus meaning stone and used for counting. Not applicable. Dark reek of bliss. Ready for. The tasks of culture.

An inlet, a very small clear center lost amid cobwebs. Light smooth as fruit. Ready to bite and sin, original. Pebbles wet, weeping willows, poplars, plum trees. The fog vast sweat. The sun too, mute. Because of the distance, a terrible thirst for love. Six thousand years ago, pictographs of trees, sacks of grain and heads of cattle. And the nature of the moon, its light borrowed at interest.

Looking at a picture of the landscape is easier than looking at the landscape. The past, upon scrutiny. Not just postwar focus, but deep and fetid. Interval eclipsed. By fog misunderstood as bird and egg, shadow by shadow. Once father and mother dissolve: dragonflies, mosquitos, missing ribs? The sign for hand in the upper right corner perhaps indicates ownership. Culture gives us these ideas. Depending on the number of chambers in the heart, trepidations of the flesh.

To understand the full clearing as the young animal turns human. Coupling curiosity with upright for speed. Hands become intelligent, economics, incorporated into body temperature. Not necessarily for the best. Raw blood, urine, faeces transformed into resemblance, contiguity and cause. And the more sensitive but sparser rods. Condition of anxious suspense converted into the tongue as home. Still, strangeness makes us shiver and retreat inside the skin.

Balked in my simulation of childhood. As consciousness flakes off, the animal soul plunges into haze. Relation of didn't perceive to didn't happen. Coercion and trimmed fingernails. Does the right to despise those outside our culture make up for the wrongs we suffer in it? Several strokes descending from heaven meant night, the principal language of Mesopotamia. Here, as in dreamlife, curiosity nestles into the fur. From humble beginnings as an accounting system. So rich a store of clay envelopes on arms raised toward gods most apt to fail us.

*Memory Tree*

AND SECONDLY, in German.

My first schoolday, September 1941, a cool day. Time did not pass, but was conducted to the brain. I was taught. The Nazi salute, the flute. How firmly entrenched, the ancient theories. Already using paper, pen and ink. Yes, I said, I'm here.

I was six or seven dwarfs, the snow was white, the prince at war. Hitler on the radio, followed by Léhar. Senses impinged on. Blackouts, sirens, mattress on the floor, furtive visitor or ghost.

And mother furious. Sirens. Hiss. The cat. My sister cried unseen. Her friend. Afraid to look. What did I know of labor (forced) or pregnant? The deep interiors of the body? I had learned to ride a bike.

The black cat. The white snow, the blue flower. A menace of a different color. Uniform movement with unsurpassed speed. Not fastidious. Not necessary for substance to be filled in deep inside.

Mother, I cried, extremely. And wolf. Exceeding the snow I was at home in, wool pulled over my eyes. O wolf. The boy who did not cry it also died. Twilight overtures.

Face fair. Black hair. Hands parsimoniously on knees. A Polish girl. In Germany? In the war? Moving along swiftly in the air between us, a continuous image. Enough of black cat panic, bells (hells, shells), of sirens, hiss of bombs.

*

A long life of learning the preceding chapter. That my soul in blue jeans, my mother in childbirth, my rabble of hopes in German, East of expectation, West of still waiting. In bed with an antidote.

Eating of the tree. Leaves falling before the fall. Through a hole in memory. The fruit puckers new problems, but doesn't quench. The orchard long abandoned.

## The Mind

SAID MY FATHER. A door open, a gray carpet, a flat dampness. A cat. A field. The means of power and coercion without which no civilization. How to possess oneself. He thought he had explained. What does "I'm frightened" mean?

A black cat. A field. All the colors of memory, however crumbled. Power, discourse, and legs. Spread in a dance too normal to stop. At pains. Not naturally fond of work.

The sun still there, the moon already in the pines. All hands in the field. Women and prisoners. War internalized as everything. A father is a father, but the super-ego is monosyllabic. The nature of touch under wraps and, like the world, folded. Can it appear in another connection?

If you tell me you're in love I understand a different order of window. Nothing avails against passion's ungainly, but luminous. Trapped in a sleepwalk. The cat both by the woodpile and in the past.

Grammar aligned according to race. Too bitterly other and taught to respect. Surplus of privation. Polish. Yiddish. Prisoners in the field. Of wheat. The cat with its sleek black pelt. Tactile parts of body. In what context? In the field, harvesting.

Let us therefore use a little nubile and strong. Bewildered, carnivore. And that from childhood. Mother in a pose of annihilation. Sexual autonomy. Does it occur? Cf. *Philosophical Investigations.* To the ends of the earth.

A simple cat by an ordinary woodpile. The body with pain and difficulty. With wallpaper of chrysanthemums. And birds of paradise. With narrow windows and stiff-backed chairs. The mind, said my father. My father in the field. Of "honor."

Spasm out of a deep-shocked realm. One could also say: I simply say it. The mind, said my father. Opaque eyes. As if sick of seeing. As if decay were mining him under the skin. Reproachful, dissatisfied. Of course we find no answer.

Or only smoke. Who lit the fire?

*Delta Waves*

WAR CAME out of the radio before I had time. To scratch on a slate. Pictograms, phonograms, determinatives. The river's edge of marsh turned solid, the year, in on itself.

Cold oozed up through the soles. Shoes always too small, bending my toes. With so many absent, how to understand human nature. Delta waves: Disease, degeneration, death, defense.

Rhythm of sleep, of the first year of life. Brackish water thickened with soot and gum arabic. My legs itched in their woolen socks. Once again following an infantile prototype.

Obedience as a time of life. Not to lose essential speed in abstraction. In the long run, an animal god does not suffice. Removed from her setting, mother paced back and forth.

I too, for no reason, walked faster and faster. Everything was exactly as it seemed. Regions compressed by growth or distorted by injury. I was "thing" because "Rosmarie" required too much lipwork from a farmer's wife.

Wiping my feet became difficult. Speaking, even in cursive script, impossible. Swallowed up by deep woods. All falling still, all lapse.

I sat on one chair and then another. As if my thought processes had no practical motives. As if I were not wishing to be part of the family next door. What happens when the shoe is on another foot?

I thought lightning and thunder meant two clouds colliding. War, a surface to live on. A relationship fixed and never failing like cause and effect. Writing begins at the edge and rolls straight toward God (red ink).

Each slap revealed a face I had not suspected. The calendar changed from moon to sun. The frequency of rhythm more important than its amplitude. Or the squeak of my shoes as I walked to the blackboard.

On the other side of sleep the scarab came into existence. Hieroglyphs beautiful enough to be the writing of gods. With birds' heads pointing the direction to read them. A net of branches denser than the woods.

Sentences enclosing and opening out. Perspective changing endlessly around the interloper. In a fragmentary passage, I held a pigeon in my hand till the trembling stopped, but not the faint, rapid heartbeat. After such intimacy, how personify the holy ghost?

*Snow*

*for Françoise de Laroque*

SOMETIMES MELTS while the seven prismatic colors in succession produce the sensation of white.

Father told stories of poisoned apples, while mother's shadow fell ever so lightly. Then the Phoenician sailors traded the alphabet for solitaire, and brain rhythms grouped in broad frequency bands.

The dark edge of the woods receded into compulsion and custom. Still, muscles resist the encouragement of descent. No shelter from a brainstorm.

But a seeming mishap may avert nakedness. Natural space lost to mirrors on the wall. Depends as much on the play of light and shadow as on the marks of graver and chisel. Mother sat elsewhere in the body.

The chemistry of the brain must be continuously adjusted to flower prints from the calendar. Not like a ship in a bottle, but awkward trompe-l'oeil. With seven dwarfs or lean years. Their violation can be made good through washing with water. Or oiling the shotgun.

Words to be revered whether or not they can be understood. A compulsion as enigmatic as layers and layers of petticoats. First remote foreshadow of a brainstorm as well as pubescent white lace apprehension. The impulse not abolished by portraits of ancestors. Or sleeping between impossible and unacceptable. The smoke is sometimes screened.

The language of the Etruscans has taken on the density of earth. Unsurveyed by geometers. Wherever two or three nerve cells are gathered together. Convulsive seizure of the day while lack of vowels drains out deep color. One after the other, mother refined the seven deadly sins. Wait until nothing is happening. Till the snow will not follow us south.

## "Shi," or The Invention of Writing

*for Per Aage Brandt*

MOTHER WORE her shiny red boots with impatience. The power of common sense disappeared through the black hole in the middle of the eye. Too many birds. The Emperor Huang-Che studied heavenly bodies. Eyes blue from watching the sky. Without compass, the tribes divided into totems and taboos.

I will now proceed with my explanation of how the margin is stripped to the last nakedness. How electrodes mean no more than the derivation of the word. How the Emperor Huang-Che studied bird and animal footprints. Members of the same totem are not allowed to enter into grammatical relations. At an angle into the blue depth of the eye. Mother thrust her chin forward so that the new violence would articulate space.

Forays in the blood where no oath could penetrate. The Emperor Huang-Che sadly waited for the tide to wash away his footsteps. The beauty of trees is useless, their representation tied to relations of production and power. If you count carefully, a comma. In the case of the mother-in-law, the rules of avoidance dangle modifiers. The Emperor Huang-Che discovered, after much study, that combining the characters for mouth and bird signifies sing; mouth and child, scream.

Grids of signs lock the planet. The Emperor Huang-Che wept through the night and, the story says, with much cause. The effect not so much related to sex as to pleasure. Not violent revolution, but native speakers. In a happy speculative mood, mother weighed mess against age, in against tension. The muscles in her neck stood out.

The scroll shows the Emperor Huang-Che wrestling with a block of ink. Because the Chinese characters have remained unchanged they have amassed a large number of meanings. *Shi*: power, world, oath, to leave, put, love, see, watch over, count on, walk, try, explain, know, be.

## The Smoke Is Sometimes Large and Colored

*for Poul Borum*

IT IS A NORTHERN COUNTRY. To which we apply close mathematical precipitation. Thought being a kind of locomotion, the subject is asked to describe exact change. A bed, a stool, a heavy-lidded from the night. Symbolic blood count propels a different satisfaction. But libido smokes outside while we talk. The work of writing. Not to embroider but out of the blue. With delight, the Abbé Jaugeon locked letters in a grid.

Harsh, brief, poor. One word before other spatial ideas. Or the eye chart for boldness and freedom. Pushed sideways in time, desire quickens, even when directed toward a cut above. Yesterday was to the left. No wonder father's puny tobacco plants never got off the ground. Manuals by hand though an iron bed and copper plate would print large sheets.

Snow cargo. Intensive or. The process of scanning relaxes when the knife is found. Spinning and dizzy. After a trudge through our own vast emptiness. Every individual shows a mixture of biological sex with cycles per second. A union of activity and under water. Day follows day with the certainty initiated by the rotary press.

Rises from a complication of visual and tactile. To the attic. Used for drying the puny tobacco leaves on a string. The characteristic impression of interrupted. For example a knifepoint. If you wish to understand you must follow the compact of clitoral excitation. Between elements of repressive, a staircase. How to write slowly like a man sowing a field. With mistakes. Absentminded in alphabetical order.

What happens in the brain after experience has done its utmost? Chair pulled to square eight of thought and personality? Even if we know about hope we must be present at birth. And puberty. Sit next to a new antenna for what never comes to be spoken. Later, tightly furled umbrellas. The hand for size and proportion. And an emphasis on speed love needs to come in writing.

## Composing Stick

*for Gale Nelson*

THE WAY OF experience proper is the front door. Through the back, I carry my mother's body down into sleep. My mother lode. Ingrained vocabulary. I dreamed I was human, but not sure it was possible. I refer to the factor of actuality. There being ambivalence. Charlemagne signed with a cross, which he inserted into the loops of the signature prepared by one of his scribes.

Any form of thought a spasm of pleasure if we could get at it. Mother cleared my throat. My mother tongue. Where do you put your hands when constructing a hypothesis? Or inner stairwell? The brain must be able to communicate every item of information received in one part to all its other paroxysms. Sleep at a distance. Or following a fish. A sense of unease may afflict the traveler, but the scribe must retain a steady hand.

The tide of dreams washes up in the sink. Too many chairs, even at mid-day. Mother succumbed to the antique love seat. My mother of vinegar. And potatoes. If there is physical interference between these and the so-called silent areas, things are seen but not recognized. The tarot showed La Papesse, La Mort, La Tour Abolie. We may say that compulsion is beveled blindness. Initially, printing seemed more an extension of hand-writing than characters moving toward a plot.

Often our discoveries come as lucky apples. Mother in a different con-stellation of confidential. My mother of pearl. On moonless nights sur-rounded by sobs. The mechanism for opening the eyes more finely tuned. Attention prowls among privacies. Furniture, pen, ink. A flicker of worry, dilapidated in its implications.

The exaggerated application of the principle of mere neighborhood. But many people can think better with eyes closed. The back of habit. Motherproof? House of cards. The projection of unconscious hostility greatly speeded up by the introduction of paper. After a pause, I prac-ticed idleness. Down endless corridors, up winding staircases, the slow and laborious process of writing.

The elements of consciousness such as the glass reflects. Curtains, their capacity for surface. Feeling as big as the room, a child will dress up in her mother's clothes. My mother hood. Surely there are photographs to put in its place? An eyelid in the mind? When Gutenberg could not repay his debt, the banker Johann Fust confiscated all his material and hired it back to him. The hostility is cried down by an increase of tenderness, smoke blown into the room, or too sick for arrest.

# BLINDSIGHT

from *Hölderlin Hybrids*

I. *In a Doorway*

*for Lisa Jarnot*

1

The world was galaxies imagined flesh. Mortal. What to think now?
Think simple. Matter? A lump of wax? An afterglow? Or does everything
happen of its own accord? Perfect and full-bodied. No more. Observ-
able. No longer. In your eyes or line of sight. Down all three dimensions
of time. Or lock up the house. Or prophets.

\*

Here I work toward. A kind of elegy. Here a strange ceiling. "Earth fills
his mouth." I would look at you. And write you. A spell but slack at the
edge. And in the door where I stand your voice goes. Hollow.

\*

If what happened. (Happened?) Hand. Between palms. Grief. Death.
Coffee with cream. Coffee. Arms, knees and free will. And shiny. Rain-
bows.

\*

The words have detached. And spread throughout my body. Such reck-
less growth. Windbag! Want to see come full circle the wheel? To com-
ment. My own commentary till I till. My own great-granddaughter's
body?

\*

Absence. But it cuts. Repeat. Furiously Yes then No. Even a fictional
character catches a chill. Makes the heart. And cold penetrates. We do
not fall off the surface. But you, planet earth. Grow. Even as we read.
Fonder of the dark.

2

Electric bulb. How the words are. Suspended around you. And. Bones in the body.

*

In packets comes the voice. Often have I emptiness, it says. Emptiness is enough and as good as within. If your own strength carries your bones let emptiness. Lift them up to the sky. Often have I attempted the sky but it hears me not. The way corollaries are and the air. Transparent. Or not. Head wrapped in fog. But always always the earliest memory. Comes. Not as light but sluggishly. More visible must. More like a weather vane must memory. Then it revolves in feeling. In pubic hair. As if taking place.

*

Grass grows. But stalagmites too rise from below. Else out of order the world. And the more blurred, the more lost in thought. That water rises as the pipes burst we understand. Which is why the need and power to see an oak and think "oak." Is given us. And transparent flesh. And the eye, most dangerous of lenses, is given. So that we should see and imagine and think and be out of the question. So that we might weigh our answers with scales. From our eyes fallen.

*

Nowhere among the living. He remains. No razor gathers.

*

Strange things happen and unexpected. Not that I to you. Want to expose myself. And flesh touching flesh cannot explain. Innumerable cells. Spreading inward.

3

Something else it is. To leave your house and cross the Atlantic, Mediterranean, Aegean, Pacific. So many were killed. And to stand each. In a doorway. And say I don't live here.

*

In the dark leaf nerve fibers spread out and from the brain. Scatter and like flames. From the spinal cord. Stinging. And stimuli from every. By ravenous hunger overcome. Transmitting backward and forward. "Nerves" more than seven. Dwarfs hi ho off to work. And farewell to the personal. Pronoun.

*

So Mohammed. Rinaldo. Barbarossa. As divided into fragments. The emperor Heinrich. I am however mixing up the centuries. But gloom there is. In every needle, thread and cloth. Crossed the Alps and with his own voice sighed "some things ..." And his son Konrad of poison died. Hark ye the horn of the watchman at night. And hair. Away from the body grows.

*

Tendons. Muscles. Sweat. Interrupt their conversation. A man. A man by the sea. A woman. The earth and its inhabitants. Antigone. Antibody. Anathema. Discrimination, fine. What is a body? Moves. Passes water. Again and again.

*

When above the poem flames. And coal black the dream. Round the soles of your feet because. The earth pulls your body. More fiery through spheres plunged. But lovely it is the soul to unfold. And the sand burning.

4

The moon is a thin line and we see a thin line.
By Thebes and thieves! let not our names be blotted out.

*

The things that enter one's skull. But a real skeleton. With key. And describing your eyes the dark.

*

Plainly a heavy heart. Can it bring about death? Impossible to understand. But when heavy the feet yet venture out. On a path you know as long. As you live you. Cannot die.

*

A horse stares unblinking. You slap a tree trunk as if. To imprint all that's the case. Or a snow goose high above the globe. Where are you?

*

Stripes. Blue lilies. You know your neck. (Not your mind.) Is damp with sweat. And like the more solid vase both. Not without limits.

5

Narcissus, clematis, ranunculus, rancor. All the forces of flesh. And spirit clash. Shrieking birds inside your body. As when you say both Yes and No instead of music. To your own questions. As if flesh were not. Grass death should forget to mow. The ship anchored. In your head goes up. In flames and time backward.

*

You should take everything. Except your shoelaces. To heart. Which moves within the flesh. And should.

*

My friend. Take care not to die. Not be torn to pieces. And let not because we're raw. Gods lash with waves our flesh. And its muscles and fibers and vessels and fat. And with this spell move on. If indeed life is. A dream it had better be. A good one. Which goes to the heart. Yet the world is all air. My luck to hear scholars debate the word "smoke" and not. Suffocate. Whereas imaginings take shape. As though in this world.

IV. *Unaccountable Lapses*

1

What is memory? A palace? The belly of the mind? Of absence a dream? The baby in the picture I don't remember, but I remember my doll.

*

Knowledge with a flavor of thin air. The more invisible the fabric befits neighboring particles. But the sun's eaten in the sky and still. Its own body keeps. And where it is we pursue. So more like a piece of property to which I lay claim. Than a state of mind. Or androgyny. Or love of black pepper.

*

In dark ivy I sat. In the shade of an oak. Just as noon poured down and lost wax. In my ears loitered. According to tradition. A shadow fell across clear-cut narration as I followed Wittgenstein to places. Where nothing happens.

*

Even as I let wander my thoughts. The way blood cells circulate to any part of the body. Or birds keep hopping. From branch to branch. Which makes them hard to keep track of. Unless I have words that don't fall. Between the tracks.

*

How many times can one single heart beat? So many breaths deep and shallow. While the years pass without hard edges. So I could put them end to end.

2

Animals do not hunt for a story. But blind am I in my soul. A fault is embedded. And were it not for the doll I would not. Know who I am. A pocket in space expanding less rapidly.

*

A riddle is anything pure. In pure memory (what is pure memory? and where?) I might know my image. But not find a caption. Though a name of my own I have no matter what time of year.

*

So should I inward turn? Breath held long enough to show. The rim of vertical time. Molecules into slower vibrations betrayed. A flake of death off the skin.

*

Do we remain as we begin? Not to words then would thinking turn but to our first soaking sunlight. To rage raw and desperate cleaving the body. Like lightning the earth.

*

So where must I search for my childhood? Among folds of the brain at the risk of falling between? Or in my throat an acid reflux? In order to repeat? What to complete I have failed? Until there's a hole in the window where I meant to toss the stone?

3

Maybe the past is enough for the past and all its inhabitants. They need not be drawn out of retirement. But if I repeat without knowing I repeat? Am I in my own body?

*

Or is the past, like the Gods, without emotion? and gropes for our feelings lest it transparent turn? Like a woman not looked at? Fading between the pages of Grimm's *Kinder- und Hausmärchen*?

*

Meanwhile breath by breath down burns the house and under its rubble buries us. And great bodies of thought melt away. And no form identical to them ever again on the face of the earth appears.

*

Though of love and sweet of summer traces float through arteries like great ships. Carrying kits for survival since the body is practical. And only when the brain's defenses are down, as in dreams, do we drown in the pure stream.

*

The way Madame Blavatsky dipped her body in the Ganges and, says Yoel Hoffmann, said a prayer for plants. And did not consider the history of the earth and its reigns of silence and long sleep.

4

Not every fish has a jaw and many are the soft-bodied beasts our ancestors. And many forgotten beyond the shale of recall. Though their history can be read, some claim, in the cells of our body. The way language contains the layers of its development.

*

And Dante said angels have no need of memory for they have continuous understanding. But we. To enter into thought. Need a bridge.

*

But a mind obsessively drawn toward memory. Its own obstacle becomes. Like magnets pushed apart by the field they create. Or I enter the picture as a shadow because dumbly I get in the way of the light. And because I am shadow I cannot see.

*

Or the way we cut open. Heads and x-ray our chests. In the effort to find love.

*

Clustered on the tip of my tongue. Are names of species. Intermediate links that heard with their skin. Now missing for lack of. Or other reasons. While we improbable and fragile too. Head toward extinction.

*

Not hard-shell certain the outcome in the match. Of recaller and recalled. And may alter both beyond recognition. Property is not passive.

5

Sudden the song of the blackbird and touches buried desire. You are there in the sound. What goes on in the soul that we must understand and can't?

*

If the eye were a living creature, says Aristotle, its soul would be its ability to see.

*

Skin stretches below the subconscious. The song gathers. In their straying flight. Lines that carry the weight of absence.

*

This is a thirst that resembles me.

## V. *At the Sea*

1

Down to the shore. And smell of brine. Away from moss, fern, mortar, brick. Form is fatal, some say. Whereas an endless unborn surface. Without point. Of reference. Containment. Or even vanishing.

*

Here where the light is. Less hidden? Less dispersed into less things? Rolls in. White-crested. Splendor after splendor. Wall piled on wall. High as a house. And down comes crashing. Rocks. Severed heads. Centuries. And from the sand a thin veil of white recedes. And ripples and shadows and a ledge of clouds lined orange.

*

Seeing is believing. But unthreatened by the dark are words. And there take refuge. Unshadowed. And thinking too takes refuge and then its own seed of light tries to sow.

*

Pounding pounding the waves. Breath skyward drawn. Out of observable space, of muscular intuition. And the light goes on pretending that seeing is simple. That with mine own eyes have I touched. The shell in the sand. The fin of the minnow.

*

I know the creed of light. We see. On condition of not seeing. The light. Transparent we dream the immediate.

2

With such amazing speed the eye. Of Ted Williams, say. Makes contact with the ball. It does not seem tied to its body. Does this reveal the nature of vision?

*

Out at the sea I stare. As if it were the universe. Could pull the infinite into my eye. Without the rational lines of perspective. With absent wavelengths represented as imagination. Slow the eye I brought with me from Germany. And does not leave its body. Nor change the stance of distance.

*

Blue. Two kinds of. Gray. Immersion. Open. Foam. Hallucination?

*

Not toward. Not where I came from. No home beyond hard the sky limit. Away then? Seeing is leaving? The Western profile? The country whose mechanisms I understand no better than the light? And which. Like the light. Pretend they're not there.

*

We come to a limit and stop. If there is no limit we cannot distinguish. Lost and no longer. I and everything else.

*

Eyes breathe. Like open wounds.

3

Monet writes a friend he's painting "the instant." Succession stopped at success. A light his palette gives off. And color subdivided into into. On the retinal surface. Ground so fine. In each ray of light. Move motes of dust.

*

Vibrations. Speed. Weather. Whatever blue.

*

The killifish slip out of sight. Out of my mind: Sunrise. Tequila. "Ännchen von Tarau." Nails growing. Axons and dendrites. The dentist. My mother's maiden name. The ordinary physical scale.

*

And how to talk to. I don't know. The dead. We've drained the symbols so our stories be cool. But it would take. The depth of years we stand on. The sea. Frequencies out of range. And air. Insurmountable its lack of resistance.

*

Which I breathe in and breathe out. And commit my tongue to mate with the nick of time. And like a dream bone worry it. And the sound of the words has no measurable size.

*

Eyes wide open. Retinal warp. Into the distance where it stops. Being distance. The brain turns pale and like to freezing. The body takes a long time to reassemble itself.

4

Out of the word came the light. On the first day of creation. Introduced separation. From the dark. And time. In alternation.

*

The light took time. In its headlong flight. And knotted it into space. Where we pursue happiness, always belated. But the light did not remain. Unknotting the dimensions back it went. Into the word. And time's left with nothing.

*

Or the light neither returned nor issued. And needs no justification. But in the swells there's memory. Between crest and trough. Of great upheavals.

*

Refracts words. The light. Into runaway decay, instant loss. We make do with coins. And wish for slower language. Of darkness an eyeful. More local colors.

*

Eyes cross the frontiers of glass. Penetrating. Penetrated. Like lovers. And like lovers rocked loose from the ground. By the grammar of convergence or some other force. Bloodstream pulled out to sea.

*

Before slowed circulation and red sleep.

5

High tide. High above my head the water level. Rising. And thoughts float on it. Out of my depth. Their number displacing their weight. Movement in all directions, not going anywhere. A desk on the Atlantic.

*

Eye without lid. Absorptive like a sponge of undecided sex. But I'm not made for all worlds.

*

The light falls. On. Like the eye. And lingers. While its unseen colors try to penetrate under. The skin, for instance. And are blocked by the opaqueness of the body.

*

Inward the nails grow later and the mind turns on itself. Myopic poison. And great ships sail over dry land.

*

There is no clemency in the light. Or in the dark.

from *As Were*


*Vesalius as Apprentice, Fabrication*

                                          *for Mary Caponegro*

Clearly on the dissecting table the reason for parts and position ac-
quainted entire the fabric of nature

The apprentice with a syringe with skin to peel with no thought of the
old man he will be

Candle fed by the fat of life

Clearly the number position and shape and no doubt contradiction very
clearly

Patently the apprentice with his syringe given the finger with no thought
of ill of infirm of the chamberpot he might need by his bed

Wrongly remembered becomes murky smoke

Then the function of muscles imagine through glass where thickens ac-
quainted entire pockets permitting a limb

Tourniquets did little to stay the

The apprentice with his syringe with light bright as advertising with no
thought of his funeral of who might weep who send flowers

Death extends as far as the smoke continues

Hand in pocket hardly one for dissecting the living clearly the contra-
dictions are many

## Hernando De Soto as Writer, Intrepid

Sailed from Havana, cast seven days' anchor, discovered the Mississippi—to the surprise of the red men not in a rush to become deckhands. The writer at her desk begins with a convulsion of the thumb and index finger or, sometimes, the big toe. She wants his body. To change geometry just as space curves near a large mass.

Talks too much, book on the floor, spine torn, vain, boastful, sand in her mouth, drinks ink, beside herself with

Reasonably certain he looked across the river, maybe stopped swearing, but did he look at the muddy current, how it rushes and overspreads the swamps? As the writer's doubts sooner or later spread across her fleet of nine vessels. We avoid these spasms by holding on to definitions of the rigid body and three meals a day.

Sudden calamity, carried off, the current, eddies, rafts, ridges, too clotted for narrative, rings under her eyes, too slow for a long life

His gaze, like most men's, on the far side of the evolutionary process, with hardware confidence. But the writer, "exceeding ready" with her words when there's already much bad grammar. And what should we interpret as physical deformation of a body, what as geometry of space?

Sandbanks, swollen waters, foam, crevasse in the levee, plastic bags, needles, telephone numbers, one silver spoon, not in her mouth

Remained to die and be buried beneath its waters, so his pact with the river not superficial. Is it worthwhile to pile on turbid water invention, hallucination, déjà vu, and a horror of death? And what is a force—I mean something to change a body?

Gators, damn it, oaths as detonating commas, sold down the river, fuck, with the lights on, cacolalia, phrases filched from

*Stein as Exact Resemblance, Exact*

Strangely simultaneous the larger the crowd at work. Strangely identical phenomena the more distant yellow splashed. Chatter angelic gesture polite honey so beguiling strangely.

Did spend time to be meant among opaque could save the sentence. Did spend into the world once an angry man is no wiser a sentence. Goes on elsewhere dragged we think along the ground did spend.

When we listen astounding no longer listen the midst of bewailing. When we listen a temporary umbrella a candle a quart of sleep. Of swept water flushed out of sound out of sound when we.

Plenty of space plenty of ordinary plenty of present. With plenty of dust to cover a single event and no comma it's nothing. Means nothing in spite of assembles assembles plenty.

## Musil as Potential, Aloof

His body is the distance that separates him from his object. A definition must precede measurement and reminiscences. Everyday actions, like she came down the stairs, multiplied by population. More than heroic energy. A slap in the face, a bite from a dog, a pair of coordinates, fictional lucky numbers.

His strange attachment to the visible even when there is no fountain. Mistake: to think the definitions cannot change. A piece of paper. Without anything written on it. She pauses, trying to remember all that might just as well be different.

He is one with the distance that separates him from his body. There is no logical objection to this. Possibility not only includes a sudden toothache, but the yet unawakened intentions of gods. Which divide the body impartially. Breath, flickering side effects, energy from the inside.

Every sensation sides with the world. In practice, a breeze through the brain. A possible experience does not equal real experience minus the value of real. Nor a woman who mails parcels to her children. Fingers feeling right under the skin.

He tries to distance himself from distance. In this connection "small area" means "on the order of the size of the earth." A possible experience, according to its followers, is something divine, a will to structure, fire, flight in quick succession. But she is dead. Separate out familiar and simultaneous.

His strange attachments. No logical objection can be advanced in small areas. So that philosophers could see what kind of unborn forest for the trees. He takes refuge in the next thing to be done. He'd go mad inside the blindspot, the place of no proof.

from *Cornell Boxes*

*Enigma Box*

Am I caught in the stare of a Medici Prince or do I hold him in the cross hairs?[1] I myself have always been quietly alert. In my dream I both stood at the stern and struggled under water, but a gun is another story. Don't step on the shards, she cries, not with bare feet, so frightening the smart missiles, the limits of time and space, the implicational character of mathematical demonstration.

Marbles, cordial glasses, soap bubbles reflect the sensual world, while around my navel there is concentrated a circular[2] red rash. I am extremely interested in failure. The beginning of art lies next to the body, transitive fissure, with high waves immediately behind. Sun, sea, severance, and people in the street, she cries, what deviance from curved diameter and straightest line.

The intimate scale of childhood also attracts hourglass, clay pipe, and intelligent collaborators. Others may prefer columns of a smaller diameter,[3] but a Mediterranean garden surrounds my Northern mind. I feel her tiny wet tongue licking my finger. The ocean, she cries, glare, wind, salt, scattered islands, limited income, it's not encounters in cabins, but chains of logical relations that compel proof.

Most remarkable, the presence of the egg. In a sea so calm not the slightest tremor suggested the tides of sexual impulse threatening the individual. The fact that we dream night after night surpasses the most heated fantasies. What lavish, wasteful refraction of light, she cries, deserted planets, desperate obsessions, do I have to invent everything all over, and without auxiliary concepts like the curvature[4] of a surface?

1  to define with accuracy, a story on shards
2  perfect, *obs.*, unease
3  through the center, and you must feed
4  the invisible if it exists across my eye

*Ice Box*

He is fascinated by the parallel seams in the ship's sails, the threads of the web. But I am not some kind of psychic casualty, I simply want to please.[1] You know, in the winter of 1835, in Russia, Marie Taglioni's carriage was halted by a highwayman? A barely perceptible, she sighs, an uncertain, and how he approached with bare feet along a line of perspective without being able to, without touching—and yet we stay on the surface and do not measure the *real diameter* through the inner parts.

If he dreams of a wooden ball with a long needle sticking through it no one in America knows more coldly accurate. The whiteness of the ship is everywhere, a short-time slice against tidal connotations. The enchanting creature was commanded to dance for this audience of one upon a panther's skin spread over the snow. Intimate turn, the unmarried moon, she sighs, so foreign, stunned senses, I panic, take flight as if the third dimension alone could tell crooked from straight.

While fervently admiring healthier possibilities, I take my florid face out of the menu and feel my armpits growing dry. What is the relation between the large particles we call elephants,[2] and the extremely small ones we call molecules[3] or fading passage? This is the counsel of despair, snow between stars. And years later, she sighs, a disappointed smile, our eyes for a, as if his double, the feeling of it gone, and the ratio changed between circumference and diameter.

He had a special star-shaped box made the more menacing. I resented this and rearranged the napkin in my lap. The motivation of biological mechanism[4] falls short of the Puritan plan. Severely ship-shape she placed a piece of ice among her jewels. First thought on waking, she sighs, dust whirling in slant light, the excessive whispers, the flight of time, but the curvature of space is the more flagrant structure.

1  the light of other days
2  elect: electrons, shimmering relation
3  feel deeply and a hint of atmosphere on sphere
4  atoms tropical, our fading passage

## Jack in the Box

*in memory of John Hawkes*

The enemies of the novel are plot, character, setting, and theme, you said, but the marquise still goes out at five, and at the stern where we were standing together but separated, it was impossible to hear the engines of the ship. The alternatives of free[1] will and causal determination do not exclude each other, though problems arise if we look for truth where definitions are needed. I heard the sudden hiss of urine. Fist through glass, you said, her legs straddling the railing, underclothes ravaged from an invisible clothesline, pollen, hollows of the body, such tension.

Everything is dangerous, you said, everything tentative, nothing certain, life jackets engulfed by crosscurrents, the thrashing of the great blades just below us and innocence in extremis. There would be contradiction only if a man could see through himself,[2] which is as impossible as knowing if a measuring rod retains its length when taken to another planet. Suppose instead we enter a period of midriffs, of second skins. Ja-Ja-Ja, you said quickly, the eye, bodily, the despotism of the uterine, odorous, earthen, vulval, convolvaceous, saline, mutable, seductive.

Can you rivet your eyes on the close-by,[3] we asked, and yet turn them toward hemispheric distances, can you crowd a spare sentence with absence and spare it? The question whether causality applies to actions of your own will is a travesty as pure and dark as a blackened negative. It's dreadful, dreadful no one has yet seen a wavelength. Of speech or suffocation, you said, white cadences, cold fire, hair like a dense furry tongue, natural lace, beetle leg, scar, a field of blood.

The enemy of pleasure, you said, is the curve of probability and flat exit. And so science must acknowledge singing in the wake of pubic darkness. A different geometry would obtain if we had rigid bodies. No turning back of time, you[4] said, unbearable sunlight, gunmetal ocean, Irish eye, glass splinters, a dream of flying and falling, a deep leap into, while the rest of us stand here, stabbed with sorrow.

1  Cf. fall, hold, lance, wheeling, dom, for all
2  and smoke five Dutch cigars
3  a single fly, buzzing
4  knife, daw, rabbit, straws, o'-lantern, in the pulpit, in the box

## Letter Box

*for Claude Royet-Journoud*

To encounter anything fully is to touch its absence, but she could not possibly wish me to kiss her lips. There's something physical about the middle of a book, a *locus of hunger*.[1] Just as the passion for seeing survives on its own sweetness, defining reverses concepts to other concepts. "Transparency of nerve," he writes, "smallness of talk, a green unruffled marble, obsessed with contiguity, periphery of language, grammar of margins."

But the center is always dissolving, hole nailed through line, sentence, and the demon of analogy. The slightness of her body was brushing against all the bulk of mine. This coordination is not arbitrary and may be explained, like the erratic course of certain stars, by a *dark companion* with strong gravitational pull. "Mouth open to earth," he writes (but will it nourish?) "obsessed with deviation, hand caught in a page, the body to come, got no tongue, will fall, the crack opens, abrupt obstacle."[2]

Something to upset the balance: *a negative dungheap, a beast dismembered on the spot.* The smallest alteration in the world of physical objects, like this photograph placed on my suitcase, produces the severest and most frightening transformations of the infinite. Whereas in physical knowledge, concepts are coordinated with particular things in a testable relation.[3] "He starts small," he writes, "hunts for his tongue, daylight doggedly, takes the place of childhood, time at a loss, hitch in the language, leaves the boat, rushes into"

A different relation to knowing, the pursuit cannot define the object of pursuit even if the road is lit by a crystal cage, lighthouse, bright red plumage, high noon. I was not surprised to be alone.[4] Certain coordinative definitions must be determined before we measure the indivisible. "I understand something quite different," he writes, "moves forward in the dark, defines the margin, bulks large in what, as if nothing, to no one."

---

1 "cramped sun"
2 "the native speech of"
3 "he sees a spot coming closer to where he's waiting for it"
4 "cold reaches its target"

# LOVE, LIKE PRONOUNS

from *Impossible Object*

## *Initial Conditions*

If thought is, from the beginning, divorced from itself, a picnic may fade before the first bottle is pulled from the basket. If you ask: Do I know what I am holding? I will offer it to you.

If a father touches the neck of his son's girlfriend, he'll fall into a Freudian sleep. If he intends to, has his palm already felt her gasp?

If you think: A young girl's a vacuum, you mean to rush and fill it. If you ask: Why? one whole chapter of life may close.

Perhaps we can't ask these questions. The traffic moves too fast. We can only throw up our arms. As in a wind tunnel?

The question: Why? is most nostalgic. In twenty years of marriage one might be in love with one another. Or with another?

Can we utter sounds and mean: young girl's neck? With one foot slightly in front of the other? Say: Come have a sandwich, and mean: best to slow down?

Could we say that listening to familiar words is quite different from a girl seen both full-face and from the side at once? Like Cleopatra? If we agree that "Have a sandwich" means "best to slow down," can we separate marriage to her brother at eleven from being carried in to Caesar in a carpet?

Either we don't move or much follows. The history of the universe predicated on ten seconds of initial turbulence?

If you ask: Where did it all begin? do I answer with a cry of distress, the tip of a triangle, a plan to picnic, a sudden toothache?

If in doubt I will offer it to you.

*Object Relations*

How differently our words drift across danger or rush toward a lover. Meaning married to always different coordinates. I married a foreigner, in one sense. In another, no word fits with another.


Your smile breaks from any point of your body. I need a more complicated picture. This falls among crow's-feet and bears no fruit. What did it try? Replace your body?


My doubts stand in a circle around us. Like visitors around the well under the house. They advise to board it up. Dampness unhinges. And decay of fish.


It would mean all night. Hands scraped on rough surmise. Remembering I too am a monster.


The objective character of statements has shifted to relations. Boiling water and the length of a column of mercury? Or that you mean me when you say "you?"


When I say "we were standing close" am I saying: we were not touching? To replace a laugh. Which could be described as: wish, yellowish, fish.


What if there is no well? What if language is not communication? If facts refuse coordinates? Detachment vanishes, as if thinned.


Meaning you consists in thinking of your body. There are no fish in my mouth.

*We Will Always Ask, What Happened?*

Imagine a witch in the form of a naked girl. Now say her name. Is it foreign? Was the idea of the witch complete before you named the girl? Did you go down a passage that does not exist toward a well of dark water?

Your mind makes small rudimentary motions. Because the joke is against it? Because it does not know which way to turn and keeps reviewing the field of possible action? Aches? Actresses?

I hear you sighing. Intention is neither an emotion nor yet lip-synch of longing. It is not a state of consciousness. It does not have genuine duration. I say, are you alright? Can you have an intention intermittently? abandon it like a soldier paralyzed the moment before battle? and resume it?

Could I order you to understand this sentence? just as I could tell you to run forward? into the fire?

Would the understanding cast a shadow on the wall even though a premonition is not a bullet hole?

One symptom is that space is forced into a mirror. As if the event stood in readiness behind the silver. You move your hand, and it goes the other way. Then the earth opens up and you slide down your darkest desires.

Witches were killed by fire, by water, by hanging in air, burying in earth, by asphyxiation, penetration, striking, piercing, crushing in a thousand and one ways.

What was that name you gave her?

*Isomorphic Fields*

Thinking is not an accompaniment. The fluttering of eyes and long pauses of lovers. Your attention wanders with your hands.


Unhinges the confines, and your name, trembling slightly, turns membrane. No other space permits such a glow from under the skin. As in a Florentine painting?


If my idea of thinking is modeled on breath does it imply opening my lips? Moving with the wind?


We lean toward each other and don't know what will come of it. Like an electric charge? The pull is toward loss of balance. The word "pull" already throws its shadow toward other uses, other possible attachments.


If you do not look at your feet you begin to sway. As in a gale? So while I push my image toward marriage, you stand with your legs apart and wear dark glasses.


My image, on its way to the thalamus, gives off branches forming a net. For further entanglement?


A high wind of thought? Particles with velocity but no location? Or is it geometry itself is altered next to a warm body?


The way you seem to hover above your seat. Like a hummingbird? And our gestures remain hanging, careless of the fact that visual evidence compels belief.

Is love impossible while we are in it? Do we hope it might be? Am I using words to say something quite different?

*Intentionalities*

My hand moves along your thigh. When we describe intentions, is the ventriloquist taken over by the dummy? Or pretending to be a ghost?

Instead of "I meant you," I could say, "We walked through wet streets, toward a dark well." But could I speak of you this way? And why does it sound wrong to say "I meant you by pulling away?" Like lovers caught in headlights?

If I talk of you it connects me to you. By an infinite of betweens, not by touching you in the dark. Touch is the sense I place outside myself for you to ride.

When I mean you I may show it—if we stand close—by putting my head on your shoulder. You can show you understand by describing the well under the trap door. What will you say? Don't be frightened?

The feeling I have when I mean you draws an arc of strength between my hips and the small of my back. It doesn't follow that "meaning you" is being exhilarated by terror. Of course not, you say: We need a red thread to run through, but it's entangled with space, form, future. Is this true?

It would be wrong to say that meaning you stands for a forgotten part of myself, a treatise on labyrinths, a path leading nowhere. Am I living in a shell where the sea comes in along with its sound? And drowns us?

I was speaking of you because I wanted to think about you. "I wanted" does not describe a general before battle. Nor, on the other hand, a ship heading for shipwreck. There is no way to decide whether this is an auto-biography or a manifesto.

*Enhanced Density*

Should it worry me that thought, in my sentences, seems never wholly present at any one moment? Let alone love, in my life? Even my skin has no precise shape, that is unless touched. By clothes?


There seems a brownish mist under construction. From forest fires?


My feeling for you seems to flow (like traffic?) under my skin. I want it to break through the pores and touch you. Inflict wounds so small you don't know what's killing you?


The way a word can pierce? Because of the use it has had in your life? Because it comes out of a deep well? Because war follows the opening of mouths?


You are never in front of me, like an object. And if I try to hold you sideways the melody slips away leaving a single note. Like a reflection in a shifting mirror? A phoneme escaping between the sutures of my accent?


What can I do but let my thoughts roam in the field around a word. The way desire roams through my body? It's called the meaning of the word because we cannot touch the groundwater in any other way.


Are we making an object when we make love? Do we hope it'll stay in front of us and allow us to observe it?


It may not be enough to look at a surface I love. Or parts adjacent.

from *Slowing Perceptions*


*Photo*

*for Alan Lebowitz*

definitions
abbreviate your face

you walk into abandoned

reasons
directly, driftwood
some trick of the current

eyes strange
like natural processes

openwork

between balance and precarious
a dancer
off a step

*Direction: Opposite*

opened
and expected things

a first step
I suppose tilts the imagination

a first encounter:
love, blind two-ply whirl

asymmetrical equation

we travel
even in our sleep
separately
toward already different

deaf turn of in
and out the other

slopes
to a mass of water
with neither bridge nor coming to

*Linguistic Archeology*

*for Marjorie Perloff*

a man named Freud
is learning Chinese

a woman moves
through his genital zone

from this alarm
grammatical organization

*

take another man
(young)
whose language has broken down

he has gonorrhea

*

we take Chinese
for a description of the facts
the world *is* hidden by a veil

we know that metaphor
is beautiful
and, like philosophy, leaves
everything as it is

we must fall very deep
into our memory

*

a chessboard in a painting
a feeling of
sexual immobility

the world is hidden by significance

*

take a nearsighted father

you cannot tell him
Look at that tower ten miles away and
go in that direction
out of the world

*

a woman's mouth
is a woman's mouth
a woman's voice is hidden in hair

*

he's not so
inarticulate and gurgling

the woman must be on her knees

*

a man learns Chinese
Mandarin
is not the only fruit

\*

a window
may open of its own accord
an eye
high in a tree

a woman's body parsed

\*

the young man shows his tongue
the clothes lie in heaps
on the floor

he climbs
out of a cramped position
into a
cramped position

the body is hidden

\*

but you exaggerate
a couch
can't lay a ghost

## Disaster

1

Grief it began with. And disbelief. Went and looked and went and looked. For what was no more. Scrutinized screens and saw. Nothing. The papers in the land and. Took in nothing.

*

Nothing has room. For all. No ruins can fill it. No rubble. No number of dead.

*

Like a movie. Like a comic strip. Please distinguish between. Crumbling towers and the image of crumbling towers. The image, repeated, multiplies. Locks on the plural. Crowds.

*

Our morning was mourning. Our day, frantic. Our night, fear. Up to down we prefer. And right to left. But many movements in many directions are better than how crashes a wounded boar. Through the woods where safe in the dark it used to rest.

2

A hole is. A space for thought. We fill it with flags.

*

And in their flutter we look. When a foreign language we should be required to learn. Lest elsewhere's bread give us pain.

*

We can think away towers. We can think away mountains. Once they're gone we can't. Believe it. We're made to dream dreams of fear.

*

Empty our houses. Dried up tears and bodies. Numb we sit on our chairs. Dumb. Like little children. And astonished how yet glad there are moments amid great grief.

*

We try to see. By our outfits. By our machines. Surrounded we are. By objectives. Dreams hijacked. Incomprehensible.

3

Image of a hole. Locked into the plural. Where are the villages? Trees? Animals? The people on whom we drop bombs and afterward food?

*

Often we must work with holes. In understanding. Often we must set out without knowing where. Often we must distrust narratives. Never need struggle over the meaning of death.

*

The distance between collapse and the image of collapse. Has a life of its own. And on an adverb we build war. "Virtually assumed responsibility." Someone has. It's said.

*

Image on a screen. Image in the crosshairs. Image.

*

With "collateral damage." As abstract as a percentage point.

4

Nothing is hidden. Therefore cannot see. Therefore a view of the world unimportant. Even though according to it. Every day. I brush my teeth.

*

To draw a black line. Was my intention.

*

The page is otherwise dark.

# SPLITTING IMAGE

*The Thread of the Sentence*

Etymology is one of the choices. The other, wearing your heart on your sleeveless. Cross my.

Even the straightest road conceals detours and forks. Thirst. For physical presence in tight succession. All week I concentrated on the hopeless accuracy of anxiety.

A line made to incorporate circumference. What the snow falls on. The very deep of a labyrinth, its poorly lit fortnights, its views without domain so like destiny.

Her beauty was called foreign. In relation to terms whose absence is felt. The foreign in one single thrust, absence felt elsewhere. Is self?

Not snow, but its blue shadow. Exchange of rather and disintegrating not made complex by the transfer of money. Thirst eddies.

Time is the invention of past snow. The thread I walk like a tightrope. The maze in the shape of a straight line.

Given to conclusions, I admire awkwardness in love. Open my clothes. To what stands outside my tongue.

The labyrinth is a ruse. Already passing into something else. The thread, swing, syncope life hangs by. My already share of nothing.

*The Depressive Position*

That the loved and hated aspects of the mother no longer intersect as cleavage. That after the war, segue to keening. That a choice of neuroses.

Badly drawn figures can nevertheless serve as proof. Just as inexact images will permit strict logical inference. Your father stomps into the room and demands you listen.

To experience depression as sharper perception. To geometry according. To parts to play.

Each crossing of space vows us to chance. You could walk away from your father's dirty old dressing gown. NO EXIT in the foreground introjects greed rather than solids. Could you feel in numbers?

You must not demand that the image itself be compelling, that it displace logic. That you feel strong or guilty, heat or cold, feel surface. Skin. Weaned suddenly.

Result: increased consonants of loss as have no cure and narrow compass. Each vowel akin to mourning.

To make reparation. Retracing your steps is without medical value. The depressive position: Destroy or destory. Today.

## Concrete Behavior

Acquiring the phonemes of a language is not innocent. Coins in my purse. (Intent. To appropriate the dead.)

I knock over the basket and the apples roll. Toward so many Adams. Along lines of perspective. Of lures for feeling. Of death instinct projected outward. The whole world red and yellow.

I reach for a word as if it were round and gathered the light. As if the shadow it throws were just shadow and I could step outside it.

Like money, phonemes have no reality. No weight, no color, no density of desire. An abstract value that makes possible language, lunch in a pub, and the roar of a mob out to lynch.

The apples slow down with dispersal of feeling, and eyes open. Is this called thinking? At the end of a long childhood. Taste of bruised suddenly remembered.

My words move toward you. The way my body moves toward its inter-realm. Then cannot take back its panic.

Does my feeling change when it is put into words? Does it become everybody's? How I hand you an apple is how words carry the weight of their use.

A system of color, a range of phonemes, the structure of the perceptible world. Formed by bones outside my skin. In the sweat on my face, the bread of phrases not of my making.

## Potential Reference

What bevies of consonants, regardless of surrounding sound, the mur-
muring surf of the revolving world. However infantile my babbling, my
confusions of time and place, I was out to drink foreign waters.


It's on my mother's lips the word was born. Vast possibilities deflated to
difference. Including madness, chicken sandwiches and pox. Sound shift.
Migrating stress. Water rift. Signification pulled in through the mesh.


Though I opened my mouth to take in what she said language has no
organs of its own. Already witness to another order.


What muscles could hold this motion toward lack of body, this rush
away from flesh? Could wrap (trap?) it in intimate honey, the attractions
of inertia, cockfights or sirens?


Not fish. Not fissure. Not king. Not synchronicity or dialectic, not un-
employment rate. I have premeditated sterility. Transparency of words.


Like "through." I'm only traveling.


Through money, sentences, hypotheses that don't hold water, a storm
at sea, the shallow hours of the moon. The tide recedes. Toward myths
of origins, remains of mammoths, a landbridge from Asia to alas poor
Yorick.


From which I deduce the structure of the world and the depth of mater-
nal darkness. Dissolves on my tongue the German for again-and-again,
wave-after-wave, passage, disappearance.

## The Body in the Word

*for Christopher Middleton*

It is not simple. It is opposite. Like revelation or dream. It does not lurk behind its signs. Full of fields, even when alone. Even if you rest all afternoon in a kingdom of caresses it engenders choreographies. And the voice goes deep.

Archipelagos, you write, where begin, armadillos, gloves, a cart with apples, song and pollen, rock wing, labyrinthine nests, a different game.

It is essentially. It could not be other. In the beginning absolutely. Not how the world is, it could not say. But that it exists, the word. Supreme visibility in deepest darkness. As children we kept our secret and grew old. With nudity exhausted.

As for birds, you write, beside me, abyssal glossolalia, soup, brass handles, too early in the day, formation of geese, grammar, not confession, landscape of possibles.

Nothing could be without it. It was made by us. But the nervous system speaks no known language. Roots burst out of the ground and we stumble, jolting the marriage of skeleton and flesh.

Mumblers all, you write, spit and babble, one-way sun, inch into the open, mirrors on string, scent bottles, black walls, black kitchen table, in Bamberg, touch everything.

It says nothing. It shows itself. St. Augustine was interested. Words, that is to say, no foundation. Variables crowd the lines of perception, brushing off flies, the time stolen. The body expands. Orgasm not certain.

208

# DRIVEN TO ABSTRACTION

## All Electrons Are (Not) Alike

### 1

A view of the sea is the beginning of the journey. An image of Columbus, starting out from the abyss, enters the left hemisphere. Profusion of languages out of the blue. Bluster, blur, blubber. My father was troubled by inklings of Babel and multiplication on his table. Afraid that an overload of simultaneous neural firings would result in an epileptic convulsion. The explorers' attention, like the foot of a snail, held on to the planks of their vessels, not communicating. Too intent on the physical fact, waves, whales, or poison arrows. Later, though, poured forth stories never dreamed of by the natives. As if languages were kidnapped as easily as green shady land profuse of flowers.

### 2

As Dante followed Virgil, so Columbus, Marco Polo. In those days spring came before summer, but the world was neither round nor infinite. Actual observations served to confirm what he already knew. True, clue, loop and thimbles, line up to the mast. If they did not, he rolled his eyeballs, duplicating the movement of the heavenly bodies. As if there were no transmission of impulse from cell to cell. Repair work is hard, of doubtful and intricate nature, as when a gap appears between two planks or the yarn breaks that was to haul you through the maze. What signifies? he asked. The temperature of the hand or that it held a scepter? Is it the nature of the mind to reach toward the future, to anticipate events about to happen? Stance, chance, all hands on deck. *And though I do not understande their language yet I know their king offered me his island for mine own.*

### 3

Triangulation: greed, religion, stunned surprise. Cabeza de Vaca "passed through many and dissimilar tongues. Our Lord granted us favor with the people who spoke them for they always understood us, and we them." All electrons are alike, a sunny surmise, surf, surface. Not raked by interpretation. With a flavor of asymmetry. Like the electric shock from a battery of Leyden jars administered to 700 Carthusian monks joined hand to hand. Later. Under Louis XV. No note of bruises, blunt instruments. Do we need to open and shut the window when it is transparent from the start? Or a special organ for what trickles through the hourglass? Enough to stretch your hand westward at the right moment and pull down the sun.

4

Pigafetta in the Philippines. Antonio, the exception. Amid sharks and shattered masts sharpened his pencil. For if a man has not learned a language can he have memories? Pointed at parts of the body and shaped a body of words: *samput, paha, bassag bassag,* buttock, thigh, shank, the "shameful" parts, *utin* and *bilat,* as well as ginger, garlic, cinnamon. The natives stared at the document. Unblinking. Thinking, my father thought, to distinguish its parchment body from blemishes in ink rather than title, preamble or appendices. Perhaps rather troubled with doubt. Scorching air may refute grammatical relationship as much as movement from Vicenza to Mactan, though the speed of nerve signals increases if the organism gets warm, and the creature becomes excited, perhaps delirious. Yet when an object has never been seen back home what good is a word? You have to bring the thing itself and empty your bag to make conversation.

5

Absence of meaning cracks the mirror. Yet every shard shows Columbus unfurling the royal standard on October 12, while the wind blows from the East by authority, custom and general consent. Curls, fur, furbalow, furious, further. Whereas my father was disturbed by *Being and Time,* it's in the face of uncovered nakedness Columbus issued the required proclamations. And was not contradicted. And named the islands. Was this the patter of administrative order with a gold standard? Or more self-interest than alternate fear and attention, wonder and universal grammar? Wonder is not registered in heart and blood, but occurs strictly in the brain. Hence it escapes moral categories, hatches heresies from the smell of lemons and fineness of metals. But does not leave a mark on the land, not even a patch cleared of plants not dwarfed by grafting or trained upon a trellis.

6

Take Diaz' memory congealed in time as in a chunk of amber, ambush. This city where the sun rolled over the water and through gold and silver that outshone it. Display delirious as the lovemaking of flowers. Up the 140 steps of the great pyramid. To meet you by the altar where blood is blood. The supply extravagant for all the brain's complexity. This splendor, says Diaz, of which no trace remains. Likewise closed ranks raked up to make a Spanish *noche triste*. Time does not cross precisely calibrated spaces. It flows across three months of siege. Irregularly like a river. Of blood. Noise noisome, nauseous, noxious to distant peripheries. Spears, arrows, stones, bullets, the clash of arms, the cries of warriors, war drums, conches, flutes and cymbals. Then when the pile of dead is higher than the ruins of the temple, yet does not yield electric current, when Spaniards, walking over the dead bodies, take possession (from "seat" *quasi positio*). The replete sun. At the same fixed time. Amid dead silence.

7

Merchants of language travel with paper currency. Columbus' fleet had no priest, but had a recorder. Transactions with eternity less pressing than "legality" secured by writing. The power to name. When I was ten I read Westerns by Karl May and with him crossed the border between Mexico and Canada. Columbus erased heathen names like Guanahaní. Christened the islands to become king of the promised land. As Adam, who "called the animals by their true names," was thereby to command them. San Salvador. Salvation, salve, salvage, salvo. The power to name is power. Especially when backed by guns.

8

The history of discoveries is his story of traps, mishaps, constant hurt. Of loaded dice. Outcome like reflection of clouds on ice. And once he set foot back on the continent of the past tense, the kingdom of certainty: what had Columbus found? For Ferdinand and Isabella who hoped to travel to the Indies? A packet of islands off China, vulgar pebbles a dog might worry in hot weather. Though pearls for eyes that see his steering wheel environ a round earth turning on its axis like a wheel of fortune on which more than limbs are broken. The rhythm of the midriff so closely linked to vapors of the mind. Diaphragm, frenzy, frantic, phrenology (discredited) and schizophrenia. And on the next page, my father says, a wall is still a wall, but rivers and crocodiles enlarge the landscape.

## Time Ravel

### 1

With the mind's eye. We see against the light. The way we see the dead. My father reading at his desk. Read, road, door. Remains unclear how my brain chose to store this image rather than another. Or how it veers toward the surface. Ulysses fights his way back to an Ithaca with four-lane highways. Where serfdom has been replaced by alienation, anomie, anxiety. Returns, reverts, replies. A borrowed book, the sword to its scabbard, in recompense, response.

### 2

The assumption is that the sirens have drowned in the alphabet. And been replaced by warnings, war, warp. My father's stopped reading to watch a magpie rising black and white against the sky. Memories are many. Glitter in the brain, ready to be pilfered. Does this fit my image of the real? Where the norms of social interaction have multiplied, and spontaneous acts come back as mistake? Or combustion? Natural feeling, temperament, disposition, impulse, energy all lashed fast to the mast. The rubrics of the dictionary meaning business.

### 3

The crew were afraid they would not come back, unable to close the loop time won't permit, but sometimes a ghost or shifting winds. Or the memory of a big slab of ice that a man with leather mittens splits across the middle. To reveal the time hidden within where I might not find my body for the cold. And though my mother wraps the slab in a rag before putting it in the icebox, it would not warm me enough to have a self. Same, identical. Interest, confidence, esteeem, reliance, respect. Skin, though it takes pains to remember caresses, is marked by the roads that pain takes.

### 4

Color of fables, the Indies, scarves, curves. Every island Columbus found was a vow kept toward a map with no elsewhere. High spirits and cloud theory reflect in the sea and stitch coordinates toward a flight of gulls, of stairs. America becomes a continent while numbers pass through the air, soar out of bounds. Or run from danger, flicker of fear. How can I remember my parents if I need to run my hands over my body to make sure it is there. Or lean forward to brace against *our element*, deflect its head-on force into a more general time. Where God for love of us wears clothes.

5

I can't hear my father's voice, moored as if among antipodes, articulation hindered by head hanging down and a spill of oceans. Spell, sperm, spatter, splash. If the mechanisms of subjectivity are disturbed it requires total restructuring of the world. As when I first learned that the earth turns on its axis, that spleen, n., is a highly vascular ductless gland which serves to produce certain changes in the blood. Merriment (obs.), caprice, spite, anger, malice, moroseness, melancholy. Most marked in complex civilizations where the pace of events and cordless voices exceeds all the running one can do just to stay in one place. Though silver, on clear days, is the light.

6

In haste we now blast ourselves beyond the clouds, and get lost in skies behind the sky. It's hard to rescue time from such a sight. And though they cast a shadow, perspective has no power over clouds. "Bodies without surface," they vanish the moment before the move into abstraction. The way my mother's large body evaporates before I can ask her to show me the breast I did not take. Columbus, though, Magellan, Vasco, in the name of Christ and King took firm hold of new markets. A mirror for a parrot, scissors for cinnamon, a playing card for a girl naked to the waist, a kingdom for a horse. And dust in everyone's eyes for private purchase and sale. What does it mean to recall the past if I have little sense of the present?

7

Names multiplied in the wake of caravels, clippers, communicating vessels. The spelling capricious (see spleen) as the winds. Track itineraries, track vanished and erased, track how many pages between Circe's island and Charybdis. It is not that our sensations need to match images in the brain, but that the brain needs a body for frame of reference. No matter if it be square or cant, short, squat, parts fitted together to enclose a window, door, picture or disposition of the mind. Just as emotion shows if we're ready for the future hovering at the edge of our eye.

## 8

Great beginnings too can end up a small world. Whorl, old. Set sail on the power of imagination for hearsay geographies and real dangers. With greed as secret motor. It drove them back home to cities crazy for spices and gold. In between, waves and more waves. When I think of my mother I am heavy in the pelvis with the children she wanted, and begin to sing. A complex song of if and though I never had a voice. To introduce an exclamation, condition, stipulation, untenable argument, or wish. On condition, in the event that, allowing that these long-term memories are abstractions, a different mode of thought from short-term ones. And that their differences shape my sense of time. A violet's blue as a sign of distance.

from *Driven to Abstraction*

## The One Who Counts, Who Paints, Who Buys and Sells

### ZERO, THE CORROSIVE NUMBER

Impossible. Without the idea of counting. To imagine numbers. Repeating an identical act, a particular mark. Over and over.

Like languages that express a plural by repeating the singular. Or a man with a woman, and another, and a third, a fourth.

"Etc." prolongs its shadow, its mathematical imperative. The idea that ceaselessly. A string of beads. Of follies. Of particles. Elementary? as long as the momentum. Zero as trace of one-who-counts. Is-under-the-spell. Of women? Naked. Infinite progressions. Delirious possibility. Offspring.

I dig a hole, he said, and then dig another and fill it with the soil I took out of the first hole.

A system of numbers instead ties a knot around nothing. Of abbreviations, conventions of syntax and grammar. Conventions instead of. Notch, tally-mark, or pebble. Instead of. Thou shalt not make unto thee any image, no likeness of a thing. No catalogue of ships. No list of wars.

Imagine counting emptiness. Fearless the mountain people cross the abyss on a flimsy bridge. Finger the empty space on the abacus. Has no value but colors what's around it. Like a premonition. Nudges other numbers into place. Origin and starting point. Position without precedent, as if being in the world without being born.

Once we have eaten of the fruit we cannot be. Like one who has not. Cannot vomit up the fruit and kill the ox that drank the water that put out the fire that burnt the stick that beat the dog that bit the cat that ate the serpent that crossed the coordinates.

You frame the roof as if through a window. Your eye is always the same lovely blue. In the same spot. If you connect the roof to the eye a cone of lines blossoms and intersects the flat screen you've put up. A minimum of ingenuity is required to make your marks. To represent, point for point, the surfaces of the visible world.

Among cries of swallows your dead wife's face. Recedes. And the lovely blue. Tints in front of your eyes the mist.

Many painters place the vanishing point inside a frame. Door, window, mirror, even another painting. This doubles the pull. To emphasize. High overhead. How other the dead.

Leads a double life. The vanishing point. Like zero. You agree the point represents, within the physical scene, a definite location. Location, however, vanishing toward the infinite. Your reaction to this distance is wind blowing across frozen plains.

What I am trying is to feel how this point in flight acts on the other points. Feel the creak I can't hear of the weathercock high on the steeple. wFeel the space between your body and mine squeezed out till my nipple is hard against your chest.

A flat mirror is held to the Baptistery in Florence. And the divers lines grope for agreement, illusion of truth. And stepping out the door, a figure detached and organized into a coherent image. Can I slip into the mirror? The painter's point of view? This is how I see. Incarnate.

And cannot lay my hand on your belly. For the eye is drawn out of the body. Through the centric ray. All the way to the horizon's implicit promise. And blazes blue like a demonstrative pronoun.

If zero marks the place of one-who-counts, then perspective, of the one-who-sees. Who casts his shadow. Whose soul takes flight with the point. Of view, of anchor, of vanishing. More as in death than like a bird. And from the distance watches appearance shed its weight the way a flame leaps up to meet another flame. And an alarm goes off and his soul returns to his body with increase of temperature and a pinch of salt.

And memory uncoils into *fresco* and *secco*. Like a bud into a leaf. Lest it, God forbid, be consumed in the fire. Yet even its charred residue can, by the method called *spolvero*, comfort the space your wife's face had been. For being so deep and empty now.

In Gothic painting, however, different places, different historical moments impinge without traffic jam. On one another because enfolded. In the eye of God. And out of these so very simple images, so very holy, shines a spaceless, noiseless sun. And you dare not stare too long because your vision thereafter might not refer. To objects in the world.

The way Nicolas of Cusa thought a portrait could float a monk toward things divine if the eye in the portrait held him. And, though he walk from East to West, did not leave him. Then will he marvel how, motionless, the eye moves. And in like manner moves for one who walks a contrary direction. Then he won't be able to contain. Such hallucinatory intensity. Any more than light in a bowl.

"The icon of God" such a portrait was called. Because like unto "the gaze that never quitteth." Just as the gold in the halo. Precious and immutable as He is. Could shelter His presence without annulling His transcendence. And if you understood you'd be delivered. From death congenital.

But Alberti urged, in his treatise on painting, to reject gold. In favor of white. To show the structure of holiness. Being both color and absence of color, white. Performs for God's presence. What the vanishing point does for His image, the artist. And your memory, for His image, your wife.

But more than you want to see your dead wife's face you yearn to touch. Her body. And try to find her touch in the hand that hands you a loaf of bread. But haunting is stopped by cold skin.

Is there measure on earth? Gold was thought to be. The standard against which to gauge. Not a color that vanishes in the dark. Unchanged as it replaces the ox, the loaf of bread, the bean.

No pricing system stays the light on a face, even remembered. Though the gold of the sun accelerates sap circulating in the leaf. And makes a wooden table smell of forest and recall broken weeping. And butter melts in the mouth.

Gold was precious before some prince stamped his effigy upon it. And returns to what it was. So what does the act of signifying add? A level of abstraction? "Higher?" As the human soul is said to emerge into the world with, at bottom, the spirit of an animal. But reaches up through the majesty of the revealed word toward. High up. The sphere of Nothingness. From which all worlds emanate? It's still our bottom that we sit on.

Time moves through matter. And matter decomposes. The edge of the leaf curls and yellows. The skin sags. A gap arises between "good" money, the unsullied issue of the state, and the worn (or fraudulently diminished) coins in circulation. Between face value and the frayed contours of a face in memory. A little more dead.

Because of this gap, a new form of money emerged in Renaissance states with international trade. Like Venice and Amsterdam. Not currency in the old sense. but a promise stretching time. "Imaginary" coin, a difference between is and means worthy of wars of religion. Its value globally a fixed weight of gold or silver and locally a variable amount of gold money exchangeable for it. "Bank-money," exact to the standard of the mint, the mind.

And with it a new type of transaction. Money bought and sold. Entering into relation with itself as if it too could insert the mirror. But without reflection. Or light gathered against it. Without the glow of an apple against the darker leaves. Without hold on feelings.

## Interlude: Cyclops Eye

And what is the zero that marks the place of one-who-writes? A page like snow? White without seven dwarves? The invention of a bee see? Elbowing elemen(t)s toward o.p. cues? With increasing speed and frequency? The moment the Greeks added vowels to the alphabet so that we don't have to draw on anything outside the word to construe it?

Shapes not found in nature. To take us out of body.

But I long for it. The body. Even if blue veins run from the knees to the ankles and the feet are swollen and bulge out of the shoes. And how can I long for something that is right here? A bit scattered my brain, perhaps. Not yet the bones I've carried around all my life. And by my own strength.

So I embark. On writing. With a shout at the sea around me, the surface of language. The vessel's not important, but the shout is. It brings the body. And with it the patterns I love, rhythmic, paratactic, the old oral forms, repetition, alliteration. And if I don't use formulae and proverbs I at least play among their echoes in the inner ear.

Words that sleep in the body all night and in the daytime come out and touch you like a warm hand.

Yet all the while I sharpen my pencil to a fine point. My alphaknife to dissect the world. And remember the phoneme, an abstract value like that of zero, which makes possible the existence of language.

Intricate lines, complex, across gaps and fissures. Toward the distance needed for full understanding. Where the void opens its one eye that never closes. In the middle of the mind. Not in the proportions of body. And I'm unsure, does it make me blind or seeing.

Swallows, missiles, helicopters, wounded bodies, budding leaves, the sun rising out of the sea, streets glistening with rain, tin cans, plastic bags, armchairs, playing cards, a prisoner on a leash, chimneys, cigarette butts, colors shifting in the sky, rooftops, maples, humvees, tanks, fields of wildflowers and landmines in one big, blooming confusion.

Or the other side of language. Where I am mute and the unsaid weighs heavy. On the tip of the tongue. A foretaste of death.

from *Snapshots from the History of Nothing*

NOTHING IS ROUND

Nothing. Zero. Absence of things, of signs. Unnatural. Hover in the same space and look identical as twins. Point nowhere and like poems mean but what they say. And are but what is not. A source of horror for some, a commonplace in our speech that juggles degree zero, zero countdown, zero-sum-game and ground zero with zero option.

But zero is not nothing, not absence, not simple exclusion. A signifier with a shape that could be traced in "learned dust," on wax, on paper. A body unbound by words like nihil, niente, nada, nothing, nichts, and even zilch.

Like the phoneme that makes possible language. Neither physical nor psychological reality, but a value with an abstract and fictive importance. That enables.

The Babylonians mimicked empty space by empty space, absence by absence. So that "11" said eleven; "1 1", one hundred and one. But this gap was an inside job, had to be framed by numerals just as a pause in music must be framed by sounds. Left on its own it floats off into emptiness.

Zero knots its shape around a void. A hole a man may fall into if he can't see straight. Ring, circle (vicious?), loop that separates in from out. And is also the egg, hence generation. All and nothing in one pregnant contradiction.

As the young Elizabethan stuck his thing into her nothing he knew the serpent swallowed its tail inside Eve's body. Even before Adam knew her. And her children, begotten of nothing, are thin of substance as the air. And more inconstant than the wind that blows us from ourselves.

The Christian church too had a horror of the void. But there was Genesis. It had to be admitted that nothing was something. Had a relation to God. Was at the origin of the million of stars and the grass and beasts and rays of light. This was hard to grasp. The mere thought made you hollow like a bird bone.

St. Augustine was scared it was the devil turned night to naught. Aquinas clung to the idea that God had overcome. But St. Jerome strove to become nothing so that he could be filled with God. Huddled over the Bible, Jerome. The image of effort. Translator's invisibility as a first step toward nothingness. Though difficult to navigate: you translate word by word, you sin. Add the smallest word, you blaspheme.

As Dürer draws him, he never once looks through his study's *Butzenscheiben* at the world. Wary of the letter "l" (lust? love?) he holds on to the word. Should he look up he'd see. The icon of God's death. And next a skull, terminal of his self-deprivation, warm-blooded mammal that he is, with hair on his body and nails that grow even after death.

Miguel de Molinos, Quietist, likewise embraced nothing as a form of being. As if he could press it to his chest and lead it in a tango. And the bishops who said nothing's not to dance with, may their name be forgotten. Killed off his will to thicken the argument. So God would have to work His own ways upon Miguel, the passive and sinless. Whose eyes were on the emptiness behind the clouds. Was this worth dying for, in a prison of the Inquisition?

And how did Meister Eckhart escape the charge of heresy? Not only not finite, not mortal, not describable, not changeable, not temporal, not anything was his Godhead. But so far past all being that He must be. Absolute nothing. *Nihte*. The Nothing that is the ground of being. Not something you can hold. A here that is not here. An absence we feel and don't feel.

Once you open your mouth to the idea of nothing there is danger. Once you pronounce possible the absence of God you could fall through it. Then what happens to His eye on the sparrow? No. No. The void was to be (religiously) avoided.

But zero had come and worked its mischief all through Christian Europe. And the pair of "nothing" and "everything" was too enticing to be kept under a doctrinal lid. The scientists (in the 17th century) worked hard to accommodate concepts of nothing: the physical vacuum—a hole in the life-giving plenum of air. "Empty space"—the hole in the plenum of matter. Which, like God, had been conceived as full and indivisible.

Still a long way from what now our physicists believe, rejoining Eckhart. That nothing is the foundation of everything. That matter is constructed from it. That everything that exists is a complex enfolding of the underlying substrate of empty space. A universe of "nothing but structured nothingness."

And the rabbis? In spite of the void in the beginning, not inclined to discuss it. Or other such questions. "Whoever ponders on four things, it were better for him if he had not come into the world: what is above? what is beneath? what was beforetime? what will be hereafter?" Says the Mishnah. They stuck to interpreting any other sacred text while the great winds blew from the desert and pillars of sand rose up in the air.

Though nothing seemed, like the name of God, too fragile to be pronounced the Merkabah mystics pondered. The measure of His body. From the nails of His feet to the parting of His hair, the measure of His palm and of His toes, the dimensions of the tank He rides in, the enormous size of each of His organs, and the secret names of His limbs. And Enoch saw "the height of the Lord, without dimension or shape, and which has no end."

And one Day of Atonement, when the shofar sounded in the town of Guadalajara in the heart of Castile, there shone through the window of the synagogue the ten Sefiroth or names of God, through which the divine life pulsates back and forth. At the top, *ain* or "Nothingness," the supreme crown of the Godhead, was veiled in vapor and light so that the other nine phases of God's unfolding might be perpetually born and manifest. Nothing, having the same consonants as *ani* or "I," said "I am that I am." This supreme self-revelation of the fullness of His Being was received by Rabbi Moses ben Shemtob de Leon in prayer shawl, phylacteries, and complete devotion.

What did Rabbi Moses de Leon remember seeing? A zero? A gap become visible in existence? The Godhead divided, self-conscious, saying "I" to Himself and loving this "I" as His female form? And so creating the world?

And when night fell did Moses de Leon try to become nothing so that the words could leave his body to be put on paper? Or did he press his wife's body to his own and say no more than was necessary? And everything happened of its own accord?

*Interlude: Thought Provoking Matter*

Middle English *gramarye,* grammar, or book-learning, came to mean occult or magical lore, and through one Scottish dialect form has emerged in our present English as "glamor." Spell cast by women.

Grammar girls with words that spell power to cast spells. And provoke matter. So a black panther treads at my side and above my fingers there float petal-like flames. Words with a nimbus, a glory, a sphere of radiance. Beyond the horizon called definition.

But writing is the tool of the negative. (Through which meaning comes to us?) Effortlessly it burns all substance off the blue shapes in the east. To a density less than thinnest cloud, the word "hills." Without body. Though with form. Therefore not like God. A nothing that foams on the inkplate.

The word's power to kill—I'm not thinking of white-gloved White House memos—its violence against what it names, what it can name only by taking away its materiality, destroying its presence. Is death itself speaking.

Or is it? If the word both kills and shows "a certain slant of light on winter afternoons" that we'd search in vain anywhere else? If the word "horse" boils the animal down to the concept, and yet, in the way of hunger, hallucinates four legs, a mane, and folds of flesh? Then maybe this death is not a simple matter. And must hold a kind of life the way fog holds light?

Some say it's because the daughters of the gods came down from the heavens and mated with humans that the order of the world was thrown out of joint and opposites became entangled. So that, without the letter that kills, there is no spirit to give life?

*Absence of Origin*

BONESETTER'S LUCK: FROM ZERO TO VARIABLE

Impossible to picture nothing. Even in a mind where unicorns roam whose bodies crumble before the light. Always I find myself hiding somewhere near the edge.

It's not that nothing can come from nothing. Is it vanity, the delirious power of zero? Its exuberant potential? Of vanities? It manufactures (and without hands) an infinite of numbers we can barely imagine.

And what profit has a man? Or, for that matter, a woman? Who loves the damp detour of the body? How, among infinite numbers—exceeding the grains of sand that would fill the universe—will they know each other?

Plato's numbers had "visible and tangible bodies" even though both his eyes were fixed on the geometric roots of the world. Dog-numbers counting dogs; sheep-numbers, sheep; and bird-numbers, a flutter of wings. The *algebrista*, the Spanish bonesetter, stood ready to mend damage.

Aristotle saw abstractions, like seeing water evaporate, in his sleep. Yet still definite numbers of definite named things. A bird, a wing-blur, high, out of nothing. The vapor condenses and, in February, freezes. Dead sparrows drop from the trees.

Zero belongs to nothing. It tells no beads or tales. It counts emptiness. To declare zero the origin is to proclaim all numbers free of reference and give thanks for escape from material content. Not standing in for birds or beasts, or earrings, or guitars. Not even a cat chasing her shadow. Naked. Meaning only in relation to other signs within the system. The cat contracts her pupils and removes the picture of the world. There is no there there.

Enter the variable. A place set at the table for Elijah. Who may come suddenly. Come in the form of a beggar. Come as a herald heralding the end of days. Or not come at all. A place which, like Space in the *Timaeus,* can receive all things and yet remain without character, without color, and hard to apprehend. But creates a tango of possible equations, inequalities, identities. Algebra. Any number may dance. And without fear of broken bones.

XENOMONEY: FROM PROMISE TO TAUTOLOGY

One thirty-fifth of an ounce of gold for a dollar. The treasury was obliged. Till 1973, when the U.S. Government canceled. Such obligation. Since then exact resemblance for exact resemblance, exact same bill for exact same bill. And nothing, neither gold nor silver, in back of the mirror. (If there had been would it reveal scenes of Vietnam? Reasons of the four-fold increase in the price of oil?)

Cut loose from any fixed equivalence, the dollar sets sail and floats off-shore on market forces. Into uncertain foreign waters and computer screens. Xenomoney.

No more physical reality of a country to guarantee it. Xenomoney belongs to international business that trumps princes and States. No history or traceable origin. Like zero outside "natural" language. Anonymous. A bubble from no sinking ship.

Here creditor does not know debtor. Though they are joined together in one long chain. He cannot examine balance sheets of every link. He can only bite his fingernails. And remember a river in Poland or New Jersey.

Of course it's long since money went beyond being pure medium of exchange and infiltrated the category of "goods." Itself bought and sold. Both object and medium, thing and token, commodity and sign for a commodity, it signifies itself. As if a photograph could not only lose its reference to your dead wife but make you forget what is a face.

No more "grounding" of money signs in some prior, natural thing. Just as zero did for numbers—what "thing" could zero possibly refer to? Though Mesopotamia is split crosswise and dollarwise.

Money now creates its own significance. In the only terms available to it. Money is time. And can be bought as a financial future. According to qualities that are precisely not according. And are thought to burn open sexual parts.

To be webbed with the world I turn my back on my husband's body. I see photo-ops on a ground of oil and bourbon. And see tortured bodies. And in my head, words. Act, fact, pact, tract, intact, abstract. Hacked, racked, cracked, sacked, stacked, *nackt*.

Not a painting with perspective fixed on the infinite. Which seems peaceful because nothing can matter much from such a distance. Here, through an error in localization, the racked bodies seem lodged in my own. Belie their image nature. Time, along with the heart, stops. Between one. And the other. The eye cannot superimpose them, no matter how neatly they are stacked.

The screen image will disintegrate shortly. The bodies revert to heat. (though their traces be dated for 5730 years.) But the period where this shame remains trackable, recorded in books, could be infinite.

Power of writing. Or toughness of paper? *kein ding sei wo das wort gebricht.* No thing without words, no fact before signs, no origin, no specie, no prior body? The signs I write down here preceded by signs preceded by signs? Turtles all the way down? In signs we trust. To build balconies out over the void.

Many have thought the voice might save the body. From the abstractions we live in. Like Augustine: "we need to speak aloud into the ears." Because "the deep of the world and the blindness of the flesh." But even the voice of God walking in the garden could not make us vomit up the apple.

Or remove the mirror from our brain. Its reflection holds the secret of our existence. But we look for it in the reflected image and do not understand. We should look at the mirror itself. Should speak, as the Germans say, *fraktur.*

If there is no redemption by voice any more than by gold. If signs are irreparably dislocated from what is supposed to be their signified. How instantly then our writing, like our knowledge, becomes subject. To ever new interpretations and directions. Unsuspected futures. Off-shore versions of its previous self?

And yet. It seems outlandish that I should need legs to love Emily Dickinson. But if I can know anything at all it's because my body has made a pact with the physical world. Is plugged into it. Mindembodied intact. And yet. At the bottom of any thing I find a word that made it. And I write. Have made a pact with nothingness. Make love to absent bodies. And though I cannot fill the space they do not occupy their shadows stand between me and thin sky.

*Zero,*
*or Closing Position*

Contradict as needed.

The sequence "Driven to Abstraction" is based on Brian Rothman's *Signifying Nothing: the Semiotics of Zero,* New York: St. Martin's Press, 1987.